Best
Classroom
Practices

Best Classroom Practices

What Award-Winning Elementary Teachers Do

Randi Stone

CORWIN PRESS, INC.
A Sage Publications Company
Thousand Oaks, California

For information:

Corwin Press, Inc.
A Sage Publications Company
2455 Teller Road
Thousand Oaks, California 91320
E-mail: order@corwinpress.com

SAGE Publications Ltd.
6 Bonhill Street
London EC2A 4PU
United Kingdom

SAGE Publications India Pvt. Ltd.
M-32 Market
Greater Kailash I
New Delhi 110 048 India

Printed in the United States of America

Library of Congress Cataloging-in-Publication Data

Stone, Randi.
    Best classroom practices: What award-winning elementary
teachers do / by Randi Stone.
        p.   cm.
    Includes bibliographical references.
    ISBN 0-8039-6758-6 (cloth: acid-free paper)
    ISBN 0-8039-6759-4 (pbk.: acid-free paper)
        1. Elementary school teachers—United States—Case studies.
    2. Elementary school teaching—United States—Case studies.   I. Title.
    LB1776.2 .S86   1999
    372.11′0973—dc21   99-6079

This book is printed on acid-free paper.

    00   01   02   03   04   05   7   6   5   4   3   2

Corwin Editorial Assistant:	Julia E. Parnell
Production Editor:	Denise Santoyo
Editorial Assistant:	Nevair Kabakian
Typesetter/Designer:	Lynn Miyata
Cover Designer:	Oscar Desierto

Contents

Preface

*W*ith the advent of the Internet as a resource, I thought about all the valuable information and outstanding teachers out there. Of course, there are ways to find them, such as listservs and newsgroups, but I thought about putting it all together in a handy book. I envisioned handing an elementary teacher a book that could be considered an instant network of people, projects, ideas, and helpful tips. This is the book I envisioned.

These teachers are the ones shown in journals and magazines, the ones who win grants, fellowships, and contests. I wanted to talk with them and hear about what they are doing. I wanted to know what makes them outstanding and what they are doing in their classrooms. In effect, I wanted to eavesdrop throughout the country and poke my nose into classrooms across the United States.

This book is the result of the thought that perhaps I am not the only one who thinks like this. Perhaps every teacher thinks like this. This book is a product of sharing at its best, and the teachers you will meet in the following pages went above and beyond my submission request. I was showered with curricula, lesson plans, calendars, and more. My mailbox, fax machine, and e-mail hummed throughout the preparation of this publication.

I hope you enjoy each submission with the same enthusiasm and excitement that I did. *Best Classroom Practices: What Award-Winning Elementary Educators Do* began as a desire for an inside view of education practices in the United States. Thanks to the tremendously giving educators I had the pleasure to "talk" with via e-mail, telephone, snail mail, and so on, you too can take a peek. Enjoy the view!

Purpose

Best Classroom Practices: What Award-Winning Elementary Teachers Do is jam-packed with projects and tips from award-winning elementary teachers from all 50 states. This guide is intended to provide you with resource people who are exemplary educators. Many of these educators even included their e-mail addresses. Designed to be a helpful book for practicing as well as future teachers, this one-of-a-kind guide puts an instant network in your hands.

Who Should Read This Book

This book is for elementary educators. Although designed for teachers, this could also be a resource for administrators interested in seeing what award-winning educators are doing across the country.

Acknowledgments

I thank all the outstanding teachers across the country who took the time and energy to submit their work for this publication. Their desire to share, mixed with their excitement about the teaching profession, made this book possible.

Grateful acknowledgment is also made to the contributors for special permission to use their material. All rights are reserved.

I also thank the following reviewers: Petros Pashiardis, Michael Herman, Nancy Witherall, EdD, Sandra K. Enger, PhD, and Dr. Betty Ford.

Where to Begin

This book is a motivational guide written by teachers for teachers. Open it at any page, and take a moment to meet a teacher and share projects and thoughts. You can start in the middle, beginning, or end. Open it anywhere and be inspired!

—Randi Stone

About the Author

*R*andi Stone is a graduate of Clark University, Boston University, and Salem State College. She holds credentials for elementary education and a master of science degree in broadcast communication. She recently completed her EdD at the University of Massachusetts, Lowell. Stone is the author of a previous book with Corwin Press, *New Ways to Teach Using Cable Television: A Step-by-Step Guide* (1997).

CHAPTER **1**

Sharing Teaching Philosophies

*T*his is the place to compare your teaching philosophy with those of your colleagues.

Chapter Overview

- **Susan K. Giroux**, a first-grade teacher at Heritage Elementary School in Wilmington, Delaware, explains her multifaceted philosophy. She says that every child can and will learn and believes that teachers should never stop learning. She builds students' self-confidence to ensure that they become independent learners.

- **Kenneth Klopack**, an art educator at Funston Elementary School in Chicago, Illinois, asks, "What would civilization be without the arts?" His art philosophy includes forming partnerships inside and outside the school community.

- **Lenora Deas Akhibi**, a kindergarten teacher at William K. Sullivan Elementary School in Chicago, Illinois, has a child-centered educational philosophy. She says that she and her students travel the many roads of high expectations to reach "the land of Readers and Learners for Life."

- **Leslie Wooster Black**, a kindergarten teacher at Bay Point Elementary Magnet School in St. Petersburg, Florida, says that the climate shapes the community. She discusses how stories can help develop character and citizenship.

- **Linda Goodin Williams**, a retired science teacher from Centerfield Elementary School in Crestwood, Kentucky, shares her science/ mathematics philosophy. She says that mathematics and science are inseparable as mass, volume, and other types of measurement that are used to control variables and perform experiments.

- **Lynn Bonsey**, a sixth- and seventh-grade teacher at Surry Elementary School in Surry, Maine, believes that adolescents need voices and choices in their classrooms. She shares a sample weekly assignment sheet.

- **Michael B. Kaiser** is a fifth- and sixth-grade teacher at Pine View Elementary School in New Albany, Indiana. His teaching career is built on two premises: (a) His students are his for life, and (b) every student is gifted in some way.

My Philosophy of Teaching

Susan K. Giroux
Wilmington, Delaware

Every teacher has his or her own philosophy of teaching. I'm sure mine is like yours. My philosophy is multifaceted. It focuses on the children and what I can do to be a better teacher.

First and foremost, I believe that every child can and will learn. It doesn't matter whether the child is from an inner city, poor, learning disabled, or ADD/ADHD (attention deficit disorder/attention deficit-hyperactive disorder) or whether the child is male or female, black or white. Every child can learn. Learning is not measured against the average of the class, but by the growth the child exhibits. Take, for example, a child who doesn't know his letters and sounds while everyone else in the classroom is beginning to read. By the end of 5 months, he knows his letters and sounds and is starting to read. That's growth. It may not be on par with the others, but that child has made progress. Every child can and will learn in my classroom.

I have been teaching for more than 8 years, and this philosophy has never failed me or the children I teach. That's not to say that all children respond to my general style of teaching. They don't. It is my job, however, to make sure I'm using the appropriate learning technique to reach a child so that he or she can find some success. This leads me to the second facet of my teaching philosophy: Never stop learning.

Classes, classes, classes. I have taken many workshops, university classes, district training, and the like to learn as much as I can about how children learn and what I can do to help them become better learners. So much information about how children learn and ways to reach all children is available that there is no excuse to let children fail. The 1990s saw the most research on this area of learning.

Now is the time for teachers to acquire all the knowledge they can to help the many different children they teach every day. I have been trained in many techniques—too long to list here (nor would you want to read them)—covering mathematics, reading, science, ADD/ADHD, bilingual education, and multiple intelligences. I use these techniques nearly every day in one form or another. I can see the success in each child, and I, in turn, find success too.

The third facet of my philosophy of teaching is building children's self-confidence to ensure that they become independent learners. I want children to feel good about themselves as people and as students. When a child gains self-confidence, he or she is able to do more, try more, and have more success. I encourage children to try different learning activities and teach them that it's OK to make mistakes. Getting children to take risks in their learning is a very difficult thing to do. So many children have had a great deal of failure, either personal (home life), academic, or social, that they are afraid to make mistakes or to put themselves in an uncomfortable situation.

It is my job to show the children that I will not hurt them if they make a mistake. In fact, I encourage children to make mistakes. I model making mistakes and how I can easily fix them. The children then begin to trust me and to take chances. They know that the classroom is a safe place to experiment. A wonderful thing happens as children experiment and take chances: They become proud of themselves. They feel success, and this success breeds more success. This builds a child's self-image.

As a positive self-image grows, the need for independence blooms. The child no longer requires the teacher for approval. That approval is coming from inside the child. Isn't that what every teacher wants for his or her students—to become independent learners?

My philosophy of teaching focuses on what I do as a teacher. I expect that every child can and will learn. I keep in touch with new learning techniques and methods that will help me reach my goal of teaching every child, and I assist children in gaining self-confidence, which will lead to their independence as learners. Teaching is not an easy job, but there are ways to help you and the children be successful. This style works for me. I hope you have reflected on your style and how it works for you.

Helpful Tips

Helping Children Find Self-Confidence

One easy thing to do to help children build confidence and have them become better thinkers at the same time is to ask them questions—questions that probe deep into their thought processes. For example, when a child gives you an answer, ask the child, "How do you know that?" or "Why do you think that?" If the child doesn't know how she got the answer, then help her along by stating what she might have done to get the answer, or ask another student to comment on how the answer was derived. If you have children think about their answers, they will become better thinkers. Children who can answer difficult questions like these build their self-confidence. This questioning technique also allows you to see why children give the answers they do and can help you dismiss any misconceptions they might have.

Learning

Take one class a year. That's all. Get involved in your own learning. It needn't be a college-level class. It can be something your district offers. But the most important thing is that you learn. No matter how long you've been teaching, there is always something new to learn. You may only walk away with one new idea, but that's one more idea you didn't have before.

I teach in a school where most of the educators have been teaching for 20 years or more. The majority of those teachers take classes and workshops every summer. It is all intrinsic motivation. No one mandates it. They have a love for teaching and it shows. These teachers better themselves to better their students. They are an inspiration to me and, I hope, to you. Take a class!

Another Way to Learn

Take on a student teacher. Yes, that's what I said. I have learned so much more about my teaching style, philosophy, and techniques whenever I have a student teacher. Student teachers come to you fresh, ready to put into practice all they have learned. They have the latest and greatest ideas from the university on "good teaching practice." Sometimes they are new ideas; at other times they are twists on old ideas. I always get at least two or three new ideas from a student teacher. I also get a new perspective of myself as a teacher.

Student teachers are always asking questions such as "Why did you do that?" "What was the purpose of this?" "Have you ever done _____?" "How did it work?" These are questions we don't usually ask ourselves. These questions help me focus on why I do a particular activity. It also keeps me on my toes and challenged. I like that. It keeps me fresh. It is very easy to go stale in teaching. The teacher is alone with little positive input. Student teachers are that positive input that keeps me going. I hope they do the same for you.

Art Philosophy

Kenneth Klopack
Chicago, Illinois

My role as an art educator and fine arts advocate has me working on a "mission" at a level where the importance of cultural experiences, hands-on creativity, and the positive development of young minds concerning the arts in society is crucial.

Working with very young people is a serious proposition for anyone. Building a viable art program to affect the future of our society, our children, is a huge responsibility. I face this task head-on. I will continue to guide children and influence them to take up the arts. I will convince them that it is important to their wellness as human beings. What would civilization be without the arts, the "human thread" that holds it all together?

As a nation that leads the world, we must make it our priority to lead the world in this vital area. We must show all who look and listen how the fine arts affect the education and lives of human beings.

As it was so aptly put by John Ruskin (in the preface to *St. Mark's Rest* [1877]),

> Great nations write their autobiographies in three manuscripts— the book of their deeds, the book of their words, and the book of their art. Not one of these books can be understood without reading the other two, but of the three, the only trustworthy one is the last.

Let our legacy as a great nation and as a people show that our books will be civilized, lasting, and most of all, trustworthy to all who follow.

The working conditions of an artist must be conducive to the flow of the creativity, energy, and originality necessary to produce superlative works. I consider myself an artist with the task of influencing children about the arts. Their creativity, energy, and originality must flow if they are to be successful. Therefore, where I work and teach and where children work and learn must be a place where we are comfortable and able to allow our creative skills and experiences to flow freely.

The best way of creating an environment for art instruction is to place myself in a student's position. If I were a student who entered Room 306 for 40 minutes of art, how would I want it to look . . . to feel . . . to be? As an art teacher handling all levels of students every week, it is essential for me to form "partnerships" with many people, inside and outside the school community. I work with teachers in assessing students and examining the effects the art program has on students. I plan and create decorations for shows; prepare students, parents, and teachers for field trips; and much more. The process of collaborative communication has to remain wide open for my program to be effective.

Whenever possible, ties with community groups and organizations are made. The arts form a common denominator for groups to get involved with our school; the YMCA, the mayor's office, Cook County services, A.R.T. (Art Resources in Teaching), and many others bring ideas and activities to our door, wanting to work with us. For me, all they have to do is ask. We get involved.

Participation with others as we work on and promote the arts is the lifeblood of an educator and an artist. As long as the need exists, we will continue to spread this kind of humanistic energy to all facets of life.

A Kindergarten Teacher's Perspective

Lenora Deas Akhibi
Chicago, Illinois

My child-centered educational philosophy is rooted in the views of such notables as John Comenius and Jean-Jacques Rousseau, who laid the foundation for the student-centered curriculum. Their philosophy was based on the premise that the education of young children should follow a natural course. My views harmonize in that I have created a classroom based on nurturance, love, sharing, respect, friendship, and understanding of my young children and how they learn.

It is my belief that young children will grow in self-worth and self-confidence when they are nurtured with quality child-friendly challenges to discover and learn about self and others in a culturally diverse and challenging setting. Others, such as Johann Pestalozzi and Friedrich Frobel, also embraced the child-centered approach to learning. They observed how children learned in a natural environment of awareness, natural curiosities, doing things as well as seeing things happen, and learning through play. The child-centered approach is coupled with many challenges for the teacher, and how he or she responds may determine his or her effectiveness and, more important, the effect on student success and achievement.

It is my resolve to be the decisive factor in my classroom. In doing so, I, the teacher, will create the learning environment to reflect a supportive and friendly place for my children and their parents to want to come to each day. Making children feel safe, special, and good about themselves begins on the day they enter the classroom. By establishing this family-style setting on Day 1 and sticking to it, my children are afforded the opportunity to escape some of the negative influences they face on a daily basis at home or in the community or both. My classroom has replaced, or at most re-created, the warm, supportive family unit that seems to diminish more each year. As the faces of my children keep changing, many no longer experience any family support at all, creating a greater need for the "whole village to educate the children."

This warm and supportive classroom has a dual purpose. The warmth, love, and nurturance is coupled with a challenging learning program that demands hands-on, discovery-based learning experiences that many of my children have not had prior to coming to school. This presents a challenge to me and other teachers in similar school environments, and it is how each of us faces the challenge that determines how successful our students will become. I choose to look at what they already know and to use what is known as the foundation to build on, rather than lament over what they do not know. Once the foundation is set, I dedicate myself to using any techniques and strategies that work to ensure that my young children will be second to none in prereading, writing, mathematics, art, music, and other subject areas. This includes engaging their parents in a learning-teaching partnership. Parents are invited to work side-by-side with me in the classroom.

Despite parental involvement, I face significant impediments achieving my goals for an unparalleled learning environment coupled with a challenging educational program. I am most often hampered by the unavailability of funds. First, funds are needed for attending workshops, seminars, and conferences to stay abreast of current changes, strategies, and techniques designed to make learning fun.

Second, as new and more exciting materials become available, the cost also rises, creating a need for more funds. When needs exceed finances, teachers do what they have always done: dip into their own pockets. I do the same even though this creates an additional responsibility for me in that I have to provide the best with less. The alternative is to withdraw from my exhausted creative bank by making, begging, or borrowing materials. When my bank becomes depleted, I have been challenged to put my pencil to paper and go grant hunting.

During the past few years, I have sought and received several minigrants to supplement, enhance, and/or create special projects for my children. From these grant projects, my children have learned the importance of eating healthful foods and making better choices when shopping with their families. Moreover, they coach their families in preparing nutritional treats at home as they learn to do the same in school.

They have been enriched with singing songs and illustrating big books about these nutritious treats created in the classroom.

In addition, they learn to read graphs, distinguish singing styles, indicate and select preferences, and dramatize good literature. They have made the singing and reading connection by making several sing-along big books from their favorite songs. Many pages would be needed to explain other features of the programs I have implemented through grant monies.

As a facilitator of learning, I envision that the most important competencies I need for teaching my children are language acquisition, print awareness, reading, writing, and self-help skills. To address those competencies, I begin immersing my children in language as soon as they arrive in my class on Day 1. We begin with opening the first big book, and a magical new world opens for them, a place of new words, places, people, and things.

I have been rewarded by this firsthand experience in what language does to children even with little resource. I have heard a child picture-reading *Miss Wishy Washy* in the same way I read it to the class. It was certainly music to my ears as I watched this little boy take the words from the book and make them his own. This event gives credence to the theory that if a child can see it, hear it, and say it, he or she will learn to think it and progressively learn to write it.

Parents and other teachers and older children are invited to share our rich literature experiences by participating in the Pizza Hut/Book It Program and the Links to Literacy. I read, parents read, and student reading partners read to my children. Because books are used exclusively in my classroom, I exert much effort in obtaining good literature for the room library.

Parents are a vital component in building language fluency; they are implored to read to their children on a daily basis. My children also take home minibooks to read to their parents. This is done to encourage family reading. Family reading, in turn, will help reduce the cycle of family illiteracy. Families who read together learn and grow together. When I see my students bringing their parents to school to get books for the weekend, I say yes.

Through the pages of child-friendly, literature-based, big and small books, my children are guided through thinking skills, letter recognition, phonics, decoding words, dramatization, drawing conclusions, and making predictions. In addition, they begin to retell stories and eventually to dictate and/or write their own stories by looking at pictures or creating their own pictures.

With these experiences, my children are empowered to become early writers and publishers. Writing is initiated with language immersion because children need a resource of words for expressing their own feelings. These words are made functional in a literature-based classroom so that children are surrounded by words and learn how to use them to write in a print-rich setting.

My children are encouraged to write early by drawing pictures and by dictating to me. As they develop and progress, they are guided to research words from the big books, signs, and labels in the classroom so that they can easily access words they want to use. When children are equipped with the skills to begin decoding words for reading and writing with the supportive resources I have made available in my classroom, they are on the road to feeling good about themselves. To keep them on this positive road, I make it my personal goal to be their number one supporter, facilitator, and coach. At the completion of the kindergarten year, my high expectations pay off with confident and independent beginning readers, creative writers, and publishers.

As learners, my children and I travel the many roads of high expectations to reach the land of "Readers and Learners for Life." Down this figurative road, my children are protected from the negatives that say "no you can't" to the positives that say "yes you can." With lots of tender loving care, we say "yes" to reading, mathematics, science, social studies, music, art, and much more in an integrated learning environment. No one travels this road alone, however. By networking with other dedicated and talented colleagues and supportive administrators to share great ideas and learning, our journey will be one of lifelong learning, and I like that.

The Climate Shapes the Community

Leslie Wooster Black
St. Petersburg, Florida

Let there be no mistake: I am passionate about teaching and delighted to do it every day. The longer I am a teacher, the more refreshed

I am by the experience. I find it deeply rewarding to witness joyful children growing and learning, interacting with one another, and using tools for understanding. We as teachers must believe in the inherent goodness and worth of all children and recognize their deep need for love, respect, trust, and acceptance.

The seeds for dignity and self-worth that we plant in children's hearts and minds will forever live with them. Our example, the enthusiasm and spark of joy we bring to our classrooms, sets the tone for whatever curriculum is present. If they witness our joy in being lifelong learners, then we have served well as models. Being spontaneous and dynamic with children lets them know you will accept the same from them.

I am most rewarded when standing back and watching the children; being an observer of learners learning and not a teacher teaching; witnessing how absorbed the children are in living and thinking, sharing and risking; sensing their trust in me and in themselves; learning from them what needs to be taught; seeing them thirst for more of what we do; helping shape our goals together; seeing their talents discovered and cultivated; and witnessing an engaging, interactive classroom that is open to all possibilities and opportunities.

A classroom should be a place that offers freedom to explore while providing sufficient structure to generate learning. I believe that we should encourage children to take risks, to have courage to explore and experience new ideas, to keep time for wonder and reflection, and to grow in their capacity to concentrate. Children deserve the opportunity to search for meaning and to integrate ideas for themselves. They should be allowed freedom to take some responsibility and initiative for their own learning.

I want them to be good decision makers and to learn how to make choices with confidence. It is intelligent to ask for help when you need it, and it is OK if you make mistakes. That's a natural part of the learning process. Good teachers nurture those fragile and developing egos.

Building a sense of community is an important part of my teaching. My students and I try to help each other learn because, out there in the bigger world, we need to know how to function constructively in a group. We need to know how to let our contribution and the contributions of others work to make our communities and the world better places. The tools that help build character and community are the dynamic power of constructive human relationships, sensitivity to nurture dignity, and tolerance for diversity of ideas and creative thinking.

Because good parenting is essential for a good democracy, we need to focus more attention on the child's first teachers—those in the home. We need to provide opportunities for parents to enrich their understanding of the importance of their role in their developing child. To involve the family is to make the strongest impact on the child's progress.

The educational journey for our children must come to rest on the principles of a functioning democracy. The values we nurture in our classrooms should be ones that enable our students to become sensitive and literate citizens. We need to provide opportunities for our children to engage in the democratic process; to plan, project, and feel connected to something larger than themselves; yet, in the process, enhance themselves as individuals.

Because living in a democracy is a privilege, it carries with it a deep responsibility. We must help our children become productive citizens with the knowledge needed for understanding issues and the capacity for solving problems together. To educate our children well is at the very center of the sustaining power of a democracy. What we do in our schools needs to reflect these democratic ideals.

Building Character and Citizenship

All early primary teachers read stories to their children. To come truly prepared to deliver a story's potent message, however, is an art worth developing. Carefully selecting those stories that place children in opportunities that help develop character and citizenship can be one of the most important curricular decisions you can make as a teacher.

When good stories are told with full expression, the moral message strikes at the heart. It is as if a spell is cast as a powerful story delivers its lessons to the soul of a child. It can be transforming and everlasting, a resource for future living. Whether the tale is in quality literature or from the lips of one who possesses experience and wisdom, the path it paves in the life of the listener can help shape character and values. Character can be developed and nurtured in children. Literature and storytelling can serve as extraordinary instruments for examining issues of ethics, morals, and values.

Good stories tell all of us what we have already understood intuitively but have perhaps not yet synthesized into meaning. They help us bridge between our realities and our possibilities. We dare to dream of our own place in the future. Stories take us there.

When we need to, we can go back and revisit a story for the wisdom it provides. It reminds us of who we are and who we can become. And what does it mean to reach for your potential? In stories, we find the answers. We see the successes and failures of the characters who live for us, who surpass, reach, or fall short of their own potential. We learn their lessons and remember their consequences. Stories can come to our aid as a support when we need to face decisions.

Children need a storehouse of wisdom to serve as models of high ethical standards and to help them in examining their own lives. When we provide children with quality literature, be it fiction, legends, historical narrative, or poetry, we help them understand and value what is noble and good. Good stories captivate the imagination, stretch the limits of the mind, and create a mental picture that sticks in our conscience.

When children can pull from the resources of wisdom found in stories, they have a solid foundation for making decisions in their own lives. Opportunities to reflect, discuss, and apply issues of morality, virtue, and character help children build their storehouse for moral scrutiny.

Sometimes stories are delightful. Sometimes stories are painful. Sometimes they are powerful. They can make us cry, fear, rejoice, laugh, and wonder. They can help nurture empathy by placing us, the readers, inside the setting. We almost become other persons in other times. Perhaps we even escape who we currently are. Good stories allow the words on the page to become so vividly real and personal that we participate and identify and learn what the characters are learning. We are drawn into the story experience. (This is not like television, whose stories place the viewer in a passive, nonparticipant mode.) When life presents its crossroads, the resourceful thinker has the advantage. "I remember when ____ faced a similar problem ____. Now I can make some choices too." Our decisions and our behaviors are shaped by our thoughts.

Let your classroom be a place where stories have the prime time. Story hour is sacred. It is food for the soul and for the spirit. It can provide a cornerstone for honorable and virtuous living. Powerful stories help develop character and citizenship.

How to Make Stories the Curriculum

When stories are integrated into varied learning modalities, whether kinesthetic, visual, or auditory, through art, music, dance, or drama, they provide rich depth and become avenues for resourceful thinking and living. A child who has connected with and extended ideas about issues in stories has bonded more strongly to those issues. Stories serve as the foundation for my curriculum.

My kindergarten classroom is set up in learning centers. All activities are a direct result of the literature we are enjoying. Often, the children are encouraged to help with ideas for the centers. When I place activities there, I strive to make them open-ended and provide opportunities for children to function successfully at their own levels. Even though my children write daily in their journals, I have a writing center for activities as well.

In the reading center, I focus on lessons that nurture and develop emerging literacy skills. Close by is a comfy couch with stuffed animal story characters, a puppet stage, and flannel board stories, along with baskets and shelves of books for children to enjoy. Other centers include fine motor skills, mathematics, art, music, computer, science, geography, blocks, and housekeeping. Throughout the room hang charts of songs and poems the children know and enjoy. What you see displayed on the walls is not store-bought. It reflects the talents of the children. Their work and creative expressions are honored. It all relates to the issues in the stories we read together and discuss thoughtfully.

Each child has certain responsibilities that help our classroom function, including caring for our array of animals (birds, fish, a mouse, a guinea pig, a rabbit, and a 4-ft iguana). Kindness and helpfulness become part of our expectations for each other. The room has a certain delightful presence and provides time to learn. We are patient and recognize that we are all still learning, no matter what we already know. Each child's ability is valued and nurtured.

Every achievement threshold is celebrated with cheers, applause, and congratulations. Sticker and trinket rewards are not necessary in a system where children are intrinsically motivated. So whatever content or activity is placed in a center, every child feels the support of the community in working and learning together. I try to empower the children to make good choices independently and to be thoughtful learners in the community.

Science/Mathematics Philosophy

Linda Goodin Williams
Crestwood, Kentucky

As an elementary science teacher, I believe that I can help more elementary teachers by sharing my philosophy for teaching science/mathematics. Elementary science is very important in a student's education. Understanding how and why things happen is much more important than only knowing what and when. Science can and must be made exciting for elementary students and cannot be isolated by content. Hands-on science is a must for students. It requires careful planning and is often messy, but it makes a lasting impression.

Science lessons should be taught by questioning the students, causing them to think. The key question should lead to hypothesizing, and this will direct the activity or procedure needed to find a solution to the question. Various materials are used to explore and discover. Mathematics and science are inseparable because mass, volume, and other types of measurement are used to control variables and perform experiments.

The process skills used in a good science lesson are invaluable to everyday life. These include observing, hypothesizing, collecting and recording data, interpreting data, comparing and contrasting, drawing conclusions, generalizing, and evaluating.

National standards have been written for both mathematics and science and are very helpful in lesson design for teachers. These standards serve as guidelines for what should be taught in these content areas and should be used to ensure continuity. Copies of documents in both subject areas should be available in every school district, or they may be obtained from the National Council of Teachers of Mathematics and the

National Science Teachers Association. Many well-written commercial materials on the market follow these concepts and make planning less time-consuming.

Cooperative grouping may be practiced in many science lessons. This approach teaches students how to work with others in solving problems and that each group member has an individual responsibility that must be fulfilled. Does this sound like the real world, or do we each sit quietly in our own seats and do our own jobs in today's society?

Different learning styles are addressed through the teaching method described in the preceding paragraphs. The visual learner sees, and the auditory learner hears. The kinesthetic learner uses the sense of touch, and all the learners remember because they are doers. If the lesson includes recording and interpreting findings, then the students learn to communicate what they learn and it is reinforced. Extension activities allow students with additional needs to explore the topic in-depth if appropriate.

Students with special needs are allowed to work very comfortably within the group, learning from each group member while contributing to the total picture. Assessment may take many forms. Total group projects, individual written accounts, participation, and performance task are a few options. By using a scoring rubric that students help design and thus fully understand, they are able to evaluate their own work.

Science is the key to keeping students interested in learning if they are exposed to it and allowed to learn this way. It is not easy, but it works, and I firmly believe that it is best for students. This process affords students the opportunity to develop self-confidence and to build self-esteem. Many opportunities are available for competition on local, state, and national levels and should be made available to those students who would benefit from such exposure.

Community resources should be used whenever appropriate and include citizens from all walks of life. If the mechanic shares how simple machines work, the banker shares modern technology, the veterinarian shares animal care, and the meteorologist shares weather prediction, then earth, life, and physical science become relevant to the student. The community member becomes involved with educating students, and thus the students become active, informed citizens. This is the best public relations one can develop.

▧ Teaching Middle School Students

Lynn Bonsey
Surry, Maine

My philosophy of teaching middle school students is simple and succinct: Adolescents need voices and choices in nearly every aspect of their lives, especially in their classrooms. With my guidance, my sixth and seventh graders hammer out classroom rules, decide which books they read individually and as a group, choose what they write and how they write it, design interdisciplinary projects, and create their own assessment standards and tools. My open-ended approach works because it allows adolescents to build on their strengths and to explore their interests, plus it lets me teach in a manner that reflects current research and practice in middle-level language arts instruction.

Implementing my teaching philosophy, however, is neither simple nor as "loose" as it may sound. Creating and maintaining a dynamic learning environment where students are productive and self-directed requires me to be diligent, organized, and clear about my expectations. In other words, my students need to know where they are going, how they are going to get there, and how long the journey will take.

To accomplish this, the first thing I do on Monday mornings is distribute and review a neon-colored, three-hole-punched weekly assignment sheet. This sheet functions as an overview of the week's work and includes important reminders, specific assignment requirements, and miscellaneous messages.

By taking the time to design this organizational tool, I rarely have to deal with the "you never gave us that assignment" syndrome (which regularly afflicts middle school students), plus I do not have to invest much time or effort into tracking down makeup work for absent students. The sheet also cuts down on homework hassles between parents and students. In fact, many parents request extra "refrigerator" copies.

Perhaps the best teaching decision I ever made was to put the last four digits of my telephone number on this sheet. I tell my students that if they run into a question or a glitch with an assignment, they must call me so that we can discuss it. On average, I receive two or three student calls a week. As a result, my students build positive, strong relationships with me, and they learn how to use their voices and make the right choices to help them to be self-directed, productive learners.

Sample Seventh-Grade Assignment Sheet
OCTOBER 20, 1997

MONDAY

REMINDER: TWO book reports in TWO genres due next Thursday, the 30th. (Books need to be preapproved.)

Memorize a passage in *Romeo and Juliet.*

Keep all Shakespeare sheets in a folder. Start a table of contents for the front. You will be graded on organization and completeness.

Finish metaphor/simile worksheet.

TUESDAY

Tonight, Wednesday, and Thursday, you must either watch a commercial pertaining to the referendums and write a summary of it as explained in class or clip an ad or article out of the newspaper relating to any of the referendums (e.g., turnpike widening, transportation bond, forestry compact). If you clip an article or editorial, fill out the current event form. If you clip an ad, write a summary explaining what the issue is and what position the ad takes. Hint: Commercials for referendums often run at news time.

Write two questions for Representative Perkins.

Field trip permission slips for Thursday's trek to the jail.

Start writing directions for a game you can create related to the court system or the Bill of Rights or elections.

Shakespeare worksheets

WEDNESDAY

Referendum assignment (see Tuesday)

Shakespeare worksheets

Thank-you note for Representative Perkins

THURSDAY

REMINDER: Keep all Shakespeare sheets in a folder. Start a table of contents for the front. You will be graded on organization and completeness.

Referendum assignment (see Tuesday)

Shakespeare worksheets

FRIDAY

Start memorizing your lines for *Romeo and Juliet.*

Bill of Rights/Election game due Tuesday.

My Lifelong Promise

Michael B. Kaiser
New Albany, Indiana

I got a job! I GOT a job! I got A job! I got a JOB! I AM A TEACHER! These were my mildly excited rantings as I attempted to celebrate signing my first teaching contract back in 1972. I was prepared to change the educational establishment by myself, but why? I had just signed a legally binding contract to teach in a West End, inner-city school. Perhaps I had instantly turned into adventurer Indiana Jones.

I became a teacher thanks to all the great teachers from my past: Mrs. Davis, who showed me love; Mrs. Roy, who taught me how to read; Mr. King, who showed he cared about ME, not just my grades; Mr. Flatt, who demanded so much of me; and Dr. Claudia Crump, who saw the teacher in me and was willing to do the work to help it blossom. These great people instilled qualities in me that made me the type of teacher I am today.

My entire teaching career is built solidly upon two premises. First, for years I have lived by a verse from John 15:13, which states, "Greater love hath no man than this, that he lay down his life for his friends." As a youngster, I was always taught that the greatest thing one could do was to die for a friend. Even as a young boy, however, it was not difficult to see that one could only do that for one friend. I do not die for my students, but I have constantly laid myself down for them.

That means when they need me, no matter the time of day or night, now or 20 years down the road, I have been willing to lay down what I was doing at the time to help them get their need met, and once their needs were met, I picked up my life and went on until the next time I was needed. I have willingly spent thousands of hours at funeral homes, hospitals, student homes, and jails to keep my promise to every student on his or her first day in my class: "I care about you as a person, and I will do everything in my power to help you be a success now or 20 years from now. YOU ARE MY STUDENTS FOR LIFE, WHETHER YOU LIKE IT OR NOT. My home telephone number is . . . If you need help or just a friend, call anytime—NOW, AND FOR THE REST OF YOUR LIFE." This promise to my students has presented me with some awesome opportunities to share my love and concern with them.

Some of the most memorable times are the 2:00 a.m. talk on our living room floor with three sixth-grade boys who were in the process of running away from home; the midnight trip and 3-hour talk with a former student to convince him that life was worth living and that suicide was not the answer; a talk with a former student who returned to my class one Friday afternoon 17 years after being in my class just to talk about the hurt of his parents' divorce. You see, I can only die once for my students, but I can lay my life down for them over and over, hundreds or thousands of times, and every time shows them and their families that I am genuinely concerned for them. They know that I truly believe and live the concept of "walking the walk" and not just "talking the talk."

The second premise of my philosophy is that every student is gifted in some way, and it is worth my time and effort to help every student find that gift. Every student is worthy of my time, love, care, and concern. I sincerely believe that every student is gifted and has a valuable contribution to make to our class, so I perceive my job of teaching as being that of a genius as defined by the ancient origins of the word: to be an attendant spirit that guards and develops a person's character. As a teacher, it is my task to take individual students and show them how to develop their talents to the fullest and compensate for and overcome their weaknesses, and to guide, stretch, and hone their character.

I allow my students to reach deep within themselves and discover who they are and how they learn best. I allow my students to decide the direction and flow that learning will take. When my students help develop the learning flow, the needs of all the class learning styles are met. My class has proved over the years that students learn best when they become the teachers.

Do you want your students to be excited and involved in the projects and lessons you are presenting? One surefire method for reaching those students at the outset is to give them the goals, objectives, and criteria for the course and allow them to brainstorm the projects and activities they would want to do to match those criteria. When the students become part of the teaching process, they take ownership of their own learning. I allow my students to brainstorm 30 to 40 projects for a unit's goals, and then the students categorize the activities according to the goals they match.

Finally, the class assigns point or grade values to each project on the basis of difficulty and amount of time required to complete the project. With that complete, the class helps me establish project deadlines, and then the students contract for their grades. Students are much more willing to work toward accomplishing goals they have helped create; besides, if they are unhappy with a project, they can only complain to themselves—the project creators!

I see my classroom as an epicenter for learning. An *epicenter* is the center point of action or activity of an earthquake from which energy is released in seismic waves. Learning energy in the form of generated ideas and excitement for new knowledge and experiences radiates out from our classroom into the school, home, and community.

What happens in our class acts as a contagion that injects every part of a student's life. My students are constantly involved in teaching and sharing knowledge with others: teaching computer and research skills to first graders; sharing computer knowledge with grandparents and senior citizens who are invited to come to learn in our class; producing video documentaries on the lives of senior citizens, thus preserving a part of our heritage; documenting projects and field trips for other classes; working with their parents on science and social studies contract activities; and writing, taping, and producing biweekly newscasts for our school.

We are usually involved in thematic project learning that culminates in shared learning with the whole school, certain classes, or the community. Our projects have included turning our room into a museum of ancient civilizations; creating and giving tours of our Great Barrier Reef Museum; running our Grammar Hospital, where weekly surgery is performed on patients such as Nadine Noun and Albert Adverb; teaching our first-grade buddies the mathematics of soap bubbles; and exploring the world of "Oobleck" with younger students.

So, you are a teacher, are you? Your ultimate goal should be to become a passionate learner for that which you are about to teach. You cannot teach what you do not know, and you will not do a good job teaching if you do not enjoy what you are doing. Become a child again. Discover. Learn. Experiment. Dare to go out on a limb, and fail if necessary to learn. Let your students see you enjoying learning and being a lifelong learner. Do not be afraid to say, "I don't know," because if you

don't, it will not take your students long to discover that fact. Let your students teach you, and be assured that they will, if you will let them.

Read, read, read. Stay current with research and scientific data. Be willing to try new, innovative activities and techniques to enhance your teaching. Children learn best if they can be explorers, discoverers of knowledge. Never just give them the answer to a problem, but make them take ownership by organizing to solve the task through their own strategies.

Nothing is more powerful than students teaching students to reinforce what they have just learned. Be willing to team with other teachers in different grade levels and subject areas so that all your students can share and benefit from the expertise they have developed. As a teacher, you must become adept at helping students learn and correctly use the learning processes of testing and discovery. Provide them with lots of hands-on, brain-stretching activities that will challenge their problem-solving capabilities to the max. Show your students the relevance of learning in their everyday lives by integrating it with other subject topics they are studying. Learning can and should be exciting, challenging, relevant, and fun. Your students will only sense that as they see you engrossed in the wonder of discovery, learning something new and exciting.

Become and stay professionally involved in expanding your knowledge and areas of academic expertise. Join professional organizations and clubs that deal with areas of curriculum in which you are the most interested; become actively involved. Become involved in sharing your talents and expertise with other teachers and their students. Team up with someone who will challenge you professionally to be the best teacher you can possibly be. Learning new ideas and strategies is much more rewarding when you have someone with whom they can be shared. Be willing to network with colleagues in all academic areas.

So you want to be an awesome teacher, do you? Remember that learning is for all children, that all children can learn and participate in all activities. Never forget that learning is only as challenging, fun, and exciting as the teacher leading the class. You are the spark. You are the navigator in what should be a learning adventure. It is true that within every mature adult, a child is struggling to get out. Dare to allow that inner, childlike creativity and wonder to keep your teaching fresh, alive, and well.

Finally, and most important, being an effective teacher who will change lives requires you to get your professional and personal priorities in the correct order. Know what is most important in your life, and then be willing to stand up for it and defend it to the death. First is my family. Second are those young impressionable, inquisitive, energetic creatures called students who meander their way to Room 103 on a daily basis. To these people I have given my life. Teaching has always been and is an active lifestyle, not a 9:00-to-5:00 job.

I really believe that teachers never stand so tall as when they stoop to show that they care for their students as people, not just as academic automatons. Today's children need more than state competency criteria and high expectations. They need kind, caring, and loving professional teachers who model a deep respect for education and learning, who set an example of compassion and concern for the total student, and who can share a love for learning just from the joy that emanates from them. I daily remind myself that a teacher who only teaches the mind and neglects touching the heart has missed changing a life forever. Yes, I am a teacher. Being a teacher is not what I do. It is what I am!

CHAPTER 2

Succeeding With Reading and Writing Instruction

*T*his is the place to see what other elementary teachers are doing to succeed with reading and writing instruction.

Chapter Overview

➡ **Stacy Kasse**, a fifth-grade teacher at Taunton Forge School in Medford, New Jersey, explains how she introduces poetry to her students. The students write poetry books and participate in an annual poetry recital.

➡ **Addie Gaines**, a kindergarten teacher at Seneca Elementary School in Seneca, Missouri, describes the learning program she uses in class to help her kindergarteners grow toward conventional literacy.

➡ **Cathleen Murayama**, a kindergarten teacher at Lihikai Elementary School in Kahului, Hawaii, uses photo journals to develop children's sequencing skills, oral language development, and social interactions.

- **Cindy Montonaro** is a kindergarten teacher at Huntington School in Brunswick, Ohio. She teams up her kindergartners with fifth graders to make a class book, *Stuffed Animals Sleepover.*

- **Maggie Lee Costa**, a career education coordinator in Stanislaus County, Modesto, California, presents a "good teacher" writing sample.

- **Margaret Holtschlag**, a fourth-grade teacher at Murphy Elementary School in Haslett, Michigan, writes the *Random House Calendar for Kids.* Celebrations are connected to the learning process, and the students write about a multitude of topics.

- **Nancy J. Berry**, a first-grade teacher/principal/science and creative writing teacher (Grades K-5) at Columbia Elementary School in Logansport, Indiana, explains her "Berry" Empathetic Creative Writing Program. This includes being an empathic proofreader and friend, along with giving students personal praise.

- **Nancy Karpyk**, a second-grade teacher at Broadview School in Weirton, West Virginia, shares three of her games to reinforce vocabulary. They are Beat the Clock, Basketball, and Baseball.

- **Tammy Payton**, a first-grade teacher and Web editor at Loogootee Elementary West in Loogootee, Indiana, has a classroom library, and her students check out books daily. She describes her system in detail.

- **William Fitzhugh**, a second-grade teacher at Reisterstown Elementary School in Reisterstown, Maryland, gives an inside view of the writing process in his classroom.

Our Annual Poetry Recital

Stacy Kasse
Medford, New Jersey

Introducing Poetry

"I hate poetry!" is usually the first thing I hear out of at least one student's mouth, but poetry is very important to me . . . and eventually to my fifth-grade students, so each January we begin reading and learning about different types of poetry. Each day, a new type of poetry is introduced. The students listen to a sample poem, and then, together, the class writes one. Following this, each student practices by writing two poems: one on a specified topic, the other a free choice.

While we are writing, we are also reading. Students select five authors of poetry they enjoy and two poems. This is for the second chapter of the poetry book we write.

After all the poems are written, the students compile them. Chapter 1 consists of all the poems they have written; Chapter 2 is published poetry. The students learn how to write a dedication page and a table of contents. I always try to do this before testing because questions about the table of contents are usually included in our standardized test. The students learn much more from making a table of contents than by doing worksheets about them.

After the poetry book is assembled, the students write a short biography to go on the back cover. The front cover receives special attention as the students choose just the right name for their book. Front covers may be made from ordinary paper, although in the past students used their imaginations and were very creative. The only requirements are the following: name, date, title, and a colored graphic. White should not be showing on the front cover. The books may be bound in school, or parents may take them to a professional print shop.

Throughout the time we are writing, we are also practicing for our annual poetry recital. Each student chooses three poems—two original and one published—to present at the schoolwide assembly. We practice a great deal. The students start by introducing themselves: "Good afternoon, my name is _____, and I will be reciting three poems for you today." The students tell what type each poem is and the author's name. I tell the students that this is a type of tryout for our future play and that expression and volume really count.

The big day arrives. The students are required (requested, but highly recommended) to get dressed up—ladies in dresses or skirts and gentlemen in ties, no jeans for either. Our first-grade buddies have been alerted, and even they get dressed up and make paper roses to present. Many of my students remember being in first grade and ask all the time whether their buddies are going to do this.

We have had some fun on this day. Many students think they are not going to survive, but I assure them I have never had to pick anyone up off the floor. I sprinkle them all with Tinkerbell Dust (specially blessed by Tinkerbell when I was in Disney World) and wish them the standard "Break a leg." When I see them onstage, it is difficult to believe that these are nervous 10- to 11-year-olds. They look so poised and mannerly. I have two greeters who welcome the audience and lead the pledges. Then the show begins.

After the assembly, we all head back to the classroom, which the students have transformed into a reception area. Desks are cleared away. Tables with treats and punch are set up, and highlighted in the middle of the room are our precious poetry books. Parents, grandparents, aunts, and uncles are clearly impressed by the students' work and talent. (One year when we worked with a convalescent home, we also invited the residents. For those who could not attend, we had a "dress rehearsal" during one of our visits.)

The best part of the poetry assignment is when that one child who said at the beginning of the unit, "I hate poetry!" comes to me after the recital and whispers in my ear, "It wasn't as bad as I thought." It's then that I know we have all been successful.

Helpful Tips

People have asked me whether this project can be done with inclusion students. Let me assure you that we have done it, and that was one of the most successful years ever. The special education teacher modified the project for her students, and watching the students perform during the recital was a heart-filled experience. Do not hesitate because you may have inclusion students. Enjoy the wonderful results!

Kindergarten Literacy Program

Addie Gaines
Seneca, Missouri

As with most instruction, it is important to use a variety of methods and approaches to beginning reading. What makes sense and helps one child learn and excel may not make sense to another and may be the most difficult way for that particular child to learn. Rather than jump on the latest reading methodology bandwagon, we as teachers need to provide a variety of activities for our students.

I describe the learning program I use in my class to help my kinder-gartners grow toward conventional literacy. Part of this program was funded by a grant 7 years ago, and part is a program I designed as I completed my master's degree. The activities include the free reading and love of literature promoted by the whole language movement and a structured systematic phonics program.

The main component of my reading program is the use of big books and poems. Each week, the children and I begin a new big book and two new poems. The big books are carefully chosen with simple text, close text-picture match, and rhyme and repetition. Our shared reading time begins with rereading four poems/songs from previous weeks; then we read two poems for this week.

Each day, the leader chooses a big book from our previously read collection and we reread the story. Then, we read the book for this week. We have a minilesson each day on letter recognition, letter-sound corre-spondences, or word matching. We also review some letter-sound cor-respondences we have previously studied. Many of our big books have accompanying cassette tapes, and we listen to these too.

Four days per week, the children work in centers related to our big book theme. The listening center has small copies of the big books and cassette tapes so that the children can listen to a correct reading model. Each week, the new book is added to the collection, and all the old favorites are left in the center as choices.

In the art center, the children follow directions to make art projects related to the story. We often display these projects in the hallway to share our learning with students from other classes. The alphabet phon-ics center has puzzles, letter stamps and ink pads, Crayola letter stamper markers, games, and Do-a-Dot markers and letter patterns. The chil-dren can practice related letter and sound skills in the way of their choice.

The final center during this time is the guided writing center. Much of the time, the children take the pattern from the big book we are read-ing and rewrite it with their own ideas. We bind the books into class books that go in our reading area for reading during free reading time. At other times, we write a response to the story, such as a letter to a book character or author or a response to a related topic. The children go to each center 1 day per week. The class is divided into teams, and each team is assigned to a center each day.

Another type of learning center in the classroom is a reading workshop. The children can go to the listening center. We also have free reading time. The children can choose from any of the hundreds of books in our class to read independently, with a partner, or in a small group.

Another center is called Read Around the Room. The children are allowed to take pointers to read charts, poems, songs, and bulletin boards anywhere in the room. Because of the movement involved and the free choice, this center is a favorite among the children. The final group meets with me to read or retell a story from the predictable book they have had checked out for the previous week. I keep track of their progress with concepts of print as I listen to the children.

Each day, the children work with sequenced file folder activities that take the children from matching pictures and letters, through matching letters and sounds, to sounding out short vowel words. Each activity must be completed with 100% accuracy, and the children work at their own pace. Each level consists of 60 file folder activities, and the children earn a colored certificate for completion of each level.

We also use parts of a program called "Success in Kindergarten Reading and Writing," by Anne H. Adams. Each day, we focus on one reading skill, beginning with listing and illustrating words that contain a given letter. Other skills through which we progress include blends, final patterning (rhyming), various vowels, letter dictation, and final patterning completion. The children volunteer the words we use for the day, and we list them on the overhead projector.

Then the students are given paper, and they write and illustrate the words of their choice on the page. We file them in a notebook and send home papers quarterly so that parents can see their child's progress over time. Another component of the program is a picture word chart. A picture from a magazine is taped to chart paper, and the children volunteer words that tell about the picture. We give the chart a title and write a sentence about the picture at the bottom. We find a certain letter on the chart and circle it and identify a few words and underline them. The charts are displayed as a source for new words.

The connection between reading and writing is crucial to establish at an early age. To this end, we write a daily news chart with news from our leader. We begin with the predictable format "Today is . . . (day, month, date, year)." Then, we write news based on the current theme.

For instance, we might write about what each child likes or what the children can do or where they have gone. We practice matching and identifying letters and words on this chart too.

The children are given the opportunity daily to write about and draw whatever they wish during our writing workshop time. At first, the children begin by writing in scribbles and random letters, but eventually most children move on to writing phonetically and spelling familiar words to go with their pictures.

Our classroom is a busy place full of reading and writing activities throughout the day. The children learn the basics of kindergarten reading and writing, as well as the more important lesson that reading and writing are integral parts of the day and of their lives and that one gets to be better at reading and writing by doing just that, reading and writing!

Photo Journals

Cathleen Murayama
Kahului, Hawaii

Click! Click! Click! My camera is an extension of my right arm. It has the very important job of capturing the "precious moments" and the "ahas!" of children from the day we meet. I take a picture of each child and parent(s)/guardian when they come for their first parent conference before school begins. I then take a picture of each child engaged in an activity on the first day of school. Throughout the year, I take pictures of special events, special activities, field trips, parent involvement activities, and children engaged in learning. Some photographs are posed shots, but the majority are candid ones.

As I get the developed photographs back, the children have the opportunity to retell the events by using the photos. Sequencing skills, oral language development, and social interaction take place as the children sift through the photographs. Field trip photographs are added to the books the children have authored and illustrated as a class follow-up. Photographs are used to create books for innovations to share reading stories (e.g., a follow-up activity to the story *Yuck Soup,* by Joy Crowley, was making stone soup. As the children put in the ingredients, they said, "In go some carrots. In go some onions. In go some potatoes." I took a photograph of each addition to serve as the illustrations for the innovation.)

All the photographs are put into photo journals. These are store-bought photo albums. The photographs are removable and are arranged by event, activity, or sometimes the month. Photographs are developed in doubles so that duplicate photo journals are made. The photo journals are rotated home with the children. Each photo journal has a title or caption only. The children are encouraged to use oral language to relate the experiences to their families. At the end of each photo journal is a "Comments" page where members of each family can reflect on the experiences they had as their child shared the photo journal with them. They also share their child's interpretation or perspective of the photographs. The children get much joy from seeing themselves in the pictures. The families are delighted to be a part of our classroom as the photo journals give them the feeling of actually being there.

After each photo journal is rotated with each child, the pictures are removed and the children help sort the photographs. Each child has an envelope to store the pictures. As the children look at the pictures again, they decide who gets which picture.

At the end of the year, a personalized photo journal, "Kindergarten Memories," is compiled for each child. It contains photographs of the child's kindergarten year, along with a few work samples (e.g., picture of self drawn at beginning, middle, and end; personal journal entries; other special projects). I write a personal letter to each child and attach it to the inside back cover.

Helpful Tips

Be sure to put the photo journals together as soon as the photographs are developed. They can pile up!

Film and processing can become expensive. I take advantage of every film and processing sale. I also set aside monies from my allocation to help cover some of the cost.

The albums I use for the photo journals are the type that have clear plastic pockets so that the photographs can be slid in and out. There are about four photos on one side of a page. I have used magnetic photo albums in the past, but inserting and removing the photographs in those is more time-consuming. Also, the magnetic albums are not reusable. I can use the albums with the pockets for several years. I use as many pages as is needed for each journal and put them in a $\frac{1}{2}$-inch binder for the rotation with the children.

Start early to put the personalized end-of-year journals together! These journals are done on colored construction paper or on vellum (a heavy paper, almost as heavy as card stock). The photographs are glued onto the paper. It may help to have the children choose several photographs. If the children are at writing level, ask them to write about the photographs. Otherwise, take dictation from them.

Cross Grade-Level Writing

Cindy Montonaro
Brunswick, Ohio

One of the children's favorite activities is the "Stuffed Animals Sleepover." The children bring their stuffed animals to school and leave them overnight. The next day, the children find our classroom a mess with food wrappers, pizza boxes, empty soda cans, and so on. The animals are arranged in strategic spots. For example, one animal has its head in the potato chip bag, two stuffed animals are in the sink playing in water, and another animal is upside down in the teacher's candy jar. We discuss what might have happened.

Fifth-grade "kinderpals" help us make a class book about the sleepover. Each kindergartner dictates a story, and a fifth grader records it. Together, they illustrate a picture under the story and color it. Every child takes the book home for the entire family to enjoy.

Helpful Tips

I save as many different kinds of food wrappers as possible. If I need more, I ask food establishments in my town for donations. I have so much fun on this day. I trash the room, and the children help me clean it up. Everyone pitches in, and excitement is in the air for the entire day.

▨ A "Good Teacher" Writing Sample

Maggie Lee Costa
Modesto, California

Here is a language arts idea for the beginning of school. I always ask the students to write a description of the most important qualities of a good teacher. This assignment helps build rapport and a positive climate. Also, the result is a sincere writing sample because most young people did have a few really good teachers along the way. If they didn't, they certainly know what they prefer in their teachers. This assignment sends a signal to the students that I am interested in being that "good" teacher.

▨ Celebrating Every Day of Learning

Margaret Holtschlag
Haslett, Michigan

When I reflect on the things that have affected my teaching, I think about two things: my childhood and my writing. I grew up in a family of 12 children on the South Side of Chicago. We were an active, busy crowd, always inventing games and fun with each other. This history of creative ways to learn is part of my teaching, just as writing is integrated into all aspects of my teaching and learning. Writing has always been a part of who I am. I write every day—journals, letters, and writing projects for children.

I write the *Random House Calendar for Kids* with Carol Troja-nowski, a dear friend and fellow teacher, and each calendar lists an event and activity for children for every day of the year. Carol and I have written nine editions of this children's activity calendar, which represents more than 3,000 activities. It is a handy resource to use for things to celebrate with my students.

When Carol and I write the calendar, it is a loud, fun, dramatic time. We research several birthdays and events for each day and choose the best one to interest children. Our resources are as diverse as a huge stack of books and Internet sites. Next, we brainstorm possible activities to correspond with the date. We try to give equal exposure to many disciplines: writing, art, mathematics, science, literature, music, games, food, puzzles, dance, drama, and so on. The activities can range from academic to silly. The key is to open a curiosity for learning.

Through my writing and my teaching, I act on the belief that celebration is an essential part of learning. On the first day of school, my students and I talk about our year together as a year of celebration—the celebration of learning. I read *I'm in Charge of Celebrations,* by Byrd Baylor, and the students' first homework assignment is to bring in a photograph of something they have celebrated. It can be a birthday or a holiday, but after hearing Byrd Baylor's book, the children think about the day they learned to ride a bike or the night they saw a shooting star.

Every day throughout the year, we begin with a celebration. Once the celebration gets going, it is easy to connect it with the learning process in the classroom. Celebrations get the students talking and creating and then just naturally writing about a multitude of topics. For instance:

1. On January 21, 1993, the world's largest doughnut weighed in at 3,739 pounds in Utica, New York. It measured 16 feet in diameter and 16 inches thick. After using yarn to demonstrate the diameter of the doughnut (and learning about measurement and circumference at the same time), the students naturally had some questions about the doughnut. Who ate it? How was it cooked? Why did the people do it? This was a perfect springboard for writing letters to the people of Utica, New York. Our next steps included finding the Utica Chamber of Commerce, reviewing the format for letter writing, and composing a group letter.

2. Gutzon Borglum, designer and sculptor of Mount Rushmore, was born on March 25, 1871. After using the Internet to view pictures of Mount Rushmore and hearing a few facts about it, students met in cooperative groups to research the presidents whose heads are carved on the monument.

3. The Great American Smoke Out is held every year on the Thursday before Thanksgiving. Students needed only 30 minutes to make a collective list of 142 things to do instead of smoking. A poster listing their suggestions was displayed in the hall for the rest of the students to see.

4. The students were on their feet and moving to the music as they listened to a recording of cellist Yo Yo Ma's music on his birthday, October 7. Their writing afterward included their thoughts about how music makes them feel.

5. The dedication of the Statue of Liberty on October 28, 1886, set the stage for students to take the stance of the Statue of Liberty with a cardboard torch and book in hand, crown on head, and bedsheet draped over the shoulder. A small group of students measured the height of the Statue of Liberty (96 feet); others researched facts in books and on the Internet. One student found a firsthand account of an immigrant seeing the Statue of Liberty for the first time, and the students were set for a silent writing session in which each took on the persona of an immigrant to write first impressions of Ellis Island.

On some days, the celebrations are quite short, but when accumulated over a period of a school year, the celebrations add up to lots and lots of writing activities.

Helpful Tips

Find a few good resources and have them on hand to lessen your preparation time. Try Chase's *Annual Events* and Kane's *Famous First Facts*. Use the *Guinness Book of World Records* on CD-ROM because of its capability to search by date and, of course, my calendar, now on the Internet: http://my.voyager.net/holt/calendar.

Simple preparations and a few materials are all you need to celebrate daily with your students. Frequent, short writing experiences help your students build their skills more effectively than occasional elaborate lessons.

Vary the celebrations to address many intelligences. Some students will be motivated to write because of a mathematics connection; others might be inspired to write after having a chance to dance.

Encourage your students to take charge of the celebrations. After several weeks of writing about celebrations, the students will begin to invent their own. This can take the form of your students teaching classmates about topics of interest or planning events for the class. This collaborative action will translate into strong community building among your students and deeper learning.

Asking students to respond to a 2-minute survey to talk about what they learned from a celebration will give them the opportunity to reflect cognitively about the activities and helps tie the celebration to the learning.

Exciting, Empathic, Creative Writing Ideas, Techniques, and Activities

Nancy J. Berry
Logansport, Indiana

Creative writing is a way to express one's thoughts, ideas, and feelings. It is a unique product of one's self. Children are very creative, and they really do enjoy expressing themselves. Creative writing enables children to communicate more effectively. How do we as teachers really know what they think until we see what they say? Creative writing encourages higher level thinking skills. Children learn to listen, follow directions, think, speak in complete sentences, organize thoughts and ideas, make decisions, and develop greater proficiency in grammar, spelling, and writing skills.

Creative writing should be enjoyed and appreciated and never be graded or marked up with red ink. Each manuscript is a part of an individual. It should be handled with tender loving care and respect. I believe that a child can learn positively through creative writing. Creative writing becomes a tool to teach and reach all individuals. The magic word is *empathy.*

Empathy is feeling for others because of having similar experiences at one time or another. I named my program the "Berry" Empathetic Creative Writing Program because of the negative memories and reflections I have from my creative writing experiences. I am determined to make creative writing a positive experience and a beautiful memory for my children. Although I learned through a negative experience, the process was unacceptable to me. I wish I had had a friend who cared enough to encourage me to do my very best.

I wish I had had someone to proofread my work and to show me in a positive way how to correct my errors. I wanted to know when, where, and why I made a mistake. I wanted to be able to correct my mistakes. I believe that a mistake is a natural happening. Everyone should be given a chance to correct, to learn from mistakes with guidance, discretion, understanding, empathy, and dignity. My Empathetic Creative Writing Program was devised so that children would not feel as if their person were being criticized when making errors. I want all children to be able to express themselves freely in writing, speech, and action. They want to be told how, when, and where they can improve, but they do not need negative remarks and red ink.

Children need empathy and guidance, as well as positive remarks, when correcting errors and learning from mistakes. It is nice for them to hear "I made the same mistake when I was your age. I bet your grandpa could not do this well when he was 6 years old, or I bet the president even made a similar mistake when he was young. Gosh, you really are creative. You are smart."

Being an Empathic Proofreader and Friend

Be a friend and an empathic proofreader. After the children finish their compositions, ask them to place their stories in a designated file on the reading table. Take the story that was handed in first and have a daily empathic and positive proofreading conference with the author.

The proofreading time that I spend with every child is a precious and special time. I highly recommend this special proofreading time for all teachers and their students. It not only helps a child with her or his creative writing and spelling but also develops trust and self-esteem. It also creates a special bond that lasts a lifetime.

The teacher meets individually with each child for about 5 minutes. At this time, the teacher reads the story with the child and praises the story's creativity, style, and/or illustrations. Stories are a part of a child. Each story contains the child's thoughts and feelings. It is a product of the child's experiences, knowledge, creativity, development, and skills. Each of the stories must be enjoyed, respected, and cherished. They all are kept in a child's personal notebook and sent home at the end of the year.

Giving Each Student 5 Minutes of Personal Praise

This proofreading time is called Personal Praise Time. The children receive individual praise only because their work is individual. All receive the same amount of praise, and all are consistently reminded that they are smart and creative and that their teacher is very proud of their accomplishments.

This time is so special that the children glow all day long. The children love to write because of the great feeling of doing well and hearing it daily. Their writing improves greatly with praise. The children write easily and freely without hesitation. They write at home and bring it in to share and be proofread. The children ask their parents not to correct their stories because I need to know which spelling words need extra work.

While my students are working independently, I read each child's composition with her or him. I first say, "This is so creative. You are a great illustrator," or "I bet your grandpa did not do this well when he was in first grade." I even say that I did not know how to spell all those words when I was in first grade. I give clues on spelling when I talk with them. I often use recess time when I do not have another duty to speak with my children.

You may not be able to give 28 children 5 minutes daily, but you can give 14 children 5 minutes every other day. If you cannot give 5 minutes, give a few minutes of encouragement and empathy. Give them hope via smiles and winks. Give what you can. Time is so precious. That extra minute of saying something may make a difference in one child's life. It is worth it.

I let my children know how lucky I am to be able to read their stories. It is my opinion that my children's stories are better than some of the books in the school library. I use the names of people who children are familiar with to illustrate that they, too, have misspelled words. I label the word as upper grade-level words. I even tell them that the word is at an adult level. I always express praise and pride. This word is jotted down in a notebook to form an individualized spelling list that will be given to the child as her or his personal spelling word the following week.

Beat the Clock, Basketball, and Baseball Vocabulary Games

Nancy Karpyk
Weirton, West Virginia

The children in my class look forward to practicing their vocabulary words. Games are good tools for learning and are a lot of fun! As I introduce the new vocabulary words, the children copy them into their notebooks. Each list is written on a separate page and numbered Vocabulary 1, Vocabulary 2, and so on. During the school year, we play several games to reinforce the words.

One of my favorite games is Beat the Clock. I set a timer, allowing enough minutes to equal half the number of vocabulary lists the children will be practicing. For instance, if we are going to review six lists, I set the timer for 3 minutes. The object is to beat the clock by reciting all the lists before the timer expires. We go down the rows, and each child must read her or his word correctly. If the word is missed, I help the child correct it. To ensure that the children don't always get the same words, I ask them to trade seats with classmates. Also, I do not always start with Vocabulary 1. Sometimes we'll do lists 5 to 10 or 3 to 12. If the class beats the clock, I imprint the inside of each child's notebook with a seasonal stamp. The children love collecting these stamps.

Another vocabulary game is Basketball. To play this game, I list vocabulary words on the chalkboard. I divide the class into two teams. To earn a point and the opportunity to shoot for a basket, a child must read the word correctly and use it in a sentence. To earn an additional point, the child must make a basket. I use a small hoop and Nerf basketball that I purchased at a toy store.

Baseball is another way to have fun while reinforcing vocabulary. I write the vocabulary words on the chalkboard. I designate three bases around our classroom; the chalkboard is home base. Then I divide the class into two teams. To get on base, a child must read the vocabulary word and use it in a sentence. To advance to a base, the next team member must respond correctly. Each team gets only one out, which is an incorrect response. The other team then takes over.

▧ Our Classroom Library

Tammy Payton
Loogootee, Indiana

Have you ever wondered what to do with all the "free" books you've gotten over the years through the children's book clubs? I have made a classroom library, and my children check out books every day.

First, I created a database of my personal books and grouped them in categories according to the various themes I use throughout the year. The categories include: the five senses, emotions, farm, pioneer, Chinese New Year, Eskimo, oceans, patriotism, and major holidays such as

Christmas and Halloween. Every month, I rotate the books so that those on display are meaningful to the children.

Next, I bought self-adhesive book pockets and wrote on each pocket the theme its book belonged to. I cut tag board into $1\frac{1}{2}$-inch by $4\frac{1}{2}$-inch strips and wrote the name of the books and their authors on them. Each strip was placed inside its respective book.

I gave my children their own self-adhesive book pockets and had them decorate their personal pocket holders. These are displayed on a bulletin board. As the children browse through the library to choose their book, they remove the bookmark from inside the book and place it into their pocket holder. I can tell at a glance who has chosen which book or whether someone has forgotten to remove a bookmark from inside the book.

I gave each child a 1-gallon zippered plastic bag that has her or his name written on it. Inside the bag, I placed a paper that has a place for five book titles to be recorded as they are read by the child or parent. As each book is read, the parents indicate whether

The book was read by the child

The book was read by the parent to the child

The book was read by the child with some help from the parent

Every other page was read by the parent, then the child

I tell my children that this is not homework and that, conversely, they cannot count their reading homework as part of this activity. So how do I motivate the children to read these books?

I made a large poster chart with everyone's name on it. As each child fills up a sheet with five books (if the child is reading a chapter book, each chapter can count as one book), she or he receives a sticker on the chart. I have made a rotation of awards with this activity:

One sticker: one piece of candy

Two stickers: a toy from the treasure chest

Three stickers: one piece of candy

Four stickers: a toy from the treasure chest

Five stickers: a piece of candy and a bookmark or a large sticker badge

This rotation is repeated every five times. Where do the toys come from? At the beginning of the year, I ask parents and children to look for discarded kids' meal toys they have at home. The children bring them to school by the bags! Our treasure chest is never lacking.

The favorite books the children enjoy checking out are the ones they have written in class. With each reading theme, we create at least one class book correlating with the theme. The children are motivated to read the work created by themselves and their friends. Parents enjoy reading and seeing what their child has done in class. On the back cover of the class book, I create a comment sheet where parents can sign their names and leave comments about this book.

This classroom library provides parents with additional reading material for those who have limited books at home. It also gives parents and children motivation to take time to read together. The most successful way to teach a child how to love reading is to enjoy a book together.

An Inside View of the Writing Process

William Fitzhugh
Reisterstown, Maryland

1. *Brainstorming:* When beginning a topic for creative writing, such as Winter, a child brainstorms for all words that might be related to the topic. This encourages divergent thinking. I act as recorder and list the words on a chart. The chart is hung in the room as a reference during writing times. Some people call this a word wall. It helps the children use specific vocabulary and helps with spelling too. I also use this technique for integrating creative writing with social studies and science units. It is extremely important to make connections with all curricular areas.

The children need to write effectively about social studies (and science) topics. We also use it for seasonal writing for such events as Christmas or Hanukkah and Halloween. The children complete this brainstorming activity independently, in small groups, or as a whole class. I also lead the children to discover new words by asking prompting questions to stretch their thinking skills. We add to the word chart during the writing unit as the children discover more words.

2. *Categorizing:* As part of seat work, the children make a web about the general topic. Thus, for the topic Winter, the categories might be winter fun, winter sports, winter weather, winter clothing, winter events, animals, food, or plants. The children use the brainstorming list to complete the web. This helps them see how words are connected to each other.

3. *Picture Dictionary:* The children illustrate selected words from the brainstorming list and then write sentences for each picture. They collate the picture sheets in ABC order and staple them together to make a dictionary. This project reviews dictionary skills. Teachers might want to include other pertinent dictionary information, such as respellings, parts of speech, or synonyms/antonyms.

4. *Drafting a Story:* The children write stories on specific winter-related topics. The same words can be used in different stories. Topics for stories include Weather, Animals in Winter, Winter Sports, Winter Fun, Winter Clothing, and A Winter Disaster. Web categories make good titles. This way, the children have opportunities to write articles, realistic fiction, and personal narratives. The children need practice "sticking to the topic" (main idea), which is sometimes difficult for them. I set a minimum requirement for each child, depending on each child's ability. At the beginning of the year, the minimum requirement is five complete sentences. I edit each story with the child so that we can talk through the process. This is very time-consuming but pays off because the children become proficient authors.

5. *Publishing:* At the end of the writing unit, each child selects one of her or his stories to be rewritten with marker on chart paper. The finished stories are hung in the hall by our homeroom to be shared and read by other students. The children draw illustrations and label their pictures to be hung with the story. This is our "published" work. We usually hang up the completed creative writing before a parent lunch so that when parents come in for lunch in our room, they also have an opportunity to see our completed compositions.

CHAPTER **3**

Succeeding With Mathematics Instruction

*T*his is the place to see what other elementary teachers are doing to succeed with mathematics instruction.

Chapter Overview

- **Linda Boland**, a gifted education/mathematics specialist in Paradise Valley Unified School District in Phoenix, Arizona, shares her top 10 characteristics of a mathematics teacher.

- **Brenda Hartshorn**, a multiage primary-grade teacher (Grades 1-3), at Moretown Elementary School in Moretown, Vermont, addresses project-based learning. She shares a quilting unit that integrates children's literature, family and community connections, and mathematics concepts.

- **Cindy Montonaro**, a kindergarten teacher at Huntington Elementary School in Brunswick, Ohio, discusses experiencing sets of numbers.

- **Diane McCarty**, a fourth-grade instructor at Price Laboratory School in Cedar Falls, Iowa, received a grant for the development of a mathematics lending library for nursery/kindergarten through fifth grades. She explains this project.

➡ **Edna M. Waller**, a fifth-grade teacher at Magnolia Park Elementary in Ocean Springs, Mississippi, created "Mathville, Mississippi." This is a year-long project involving students working together, planning, constructing, and operating stores, businesses, and agencies by using necessary mathematics, social, and creative skills. Students participated in a simulation of running an actual business.

➡ **Kathi Orr**, a first- and second-grade teacher at Moretown Elementary School in Moretown, Vermont, uses mathematics in purposeful and exciting ways. Her classroom is filled with mathematics manipulatives, and she has added mathematics literature to her classroom library. She discusses her money unit.

➡ **Nancy Ann Belsky**, a mathematics teacher of Grades 5 to 8 at Westmoreland School in Westmoreland, New Hampshire, teaches her students mathematics skills through kite building.

The Top 10 Characteristics of a Mathematics Teacher
Linda Boland
Phoenix, Arizona

10. *The ability to create a safe learning environment for curiosity and risk taking:* In my classroom, students know that it is OK to make mistakes and that some of our best lessons come from sharing mistakes and "misthinking." They know that we can get into some very interesting conversations when we share our wild and illogical ideas and solutions. But this doesn't just happen. Trust is developed, and risk taking and sharing are valued.

9. *The state of being watchful and supportive of students who think they are in over their heads:* Just because students think they are in over their heads doesn't mean I cannot get them back on track. Through finding and developing areas of success, I can build their confidence to go on. But I need to be watchful! Asking for help, even asking questions, may be difficult for some students.

8. *The knack of introducing new ways to teach basic mathematics ideas and concepts:* We all have to teach the four arithmetic operations with whole numbers, decimals, and fractions at some point. It is just more interesting to have students learn them while they are also working with a minimum spanning tree or figuring batting averages or finding the best buy or comparing stock prices.

7. *The capacity to raise your comfort level with technology and a willingness to learn more:* Today's world is immersed in technology, and everyone needs to learn the basics of using a computer, whether it be an automated teller machine, a calculator, or a computer. I was fascinated when I learned how to create fractals on the computer by just using a drawing program! My students learn to use a spreadsheet. They play the "what if" game with their grades or figure exponential growth for the chessboard problem. The students view the computer as simply a tool to help them solve problems. Now we need to find even more worthwhile applications.

6. *The ability to stimulate cheerful persistence and stick-to-it-iveness in students:* In a world where we have become accustomed to instant soup, television that needs no warmup, cellular telephones, and television sitcoms that solve problems in 30 minutes, it is no wonder our students expect instant answers. I think it is important to cultivate persistence and perseverance within our students so that they see the value in pursuing problems that have more than one valid response, answers that may not come easily, or questions that may not even have a solution. That's life!

5. *The tendency to share practical, worthwhile activities and applications with students:* There is always more interest and buy-in when I can present problems the students are interested in solving or can see the value in solving for themselves personally or can apply in another situation at some other time or place in their lives. One project, "Keeping My Pet for a Year $$$," is a popular one. It is personal, relevant, and always an eye-opener for them.

4. *The stamina to keep up with the students in class, out of class, everywhere.*

3. *A style of questioning that is interesting, thought-provoking, and probing:* My favorite new word is *discourse*—ways of representing,

thinking, talking, agreeing, and disagreeing that both teachers and students use to engage in worthwhile mathematical tasks (from the National Council of Teachers of Mathematics [NCTM]). But to get discourse going, I have to ask good questions that elicit more than a word or phrase. I tell the students that I want them to answer in paragraphs. The kinds of questions I am striving for are those that aim for higher level thinking, justifying, conjecturing, projecting, inventing, and connecting. It is a skill to develop. It is not easy, but you'll improve with practice.

2. *The realization and acceptance of having/not having to have all the answers:* "I don't know, but let's explore it and try to find out" is a perfectly acceptable response from me.

1. The number 1 characteristic of a mathematics teacher is *the awareness of, and enthusiasm in, being a mathematician:* Until we as teachers begin to think of ourselves as mathematicians, our students cannot think of themselves as mathematicians. By projecting an awareness of the various intriguing aspects of mathematics (as opposed to arithmetic!) and enthusiastically drawing others into an exploration of mathematics, I can build confidence and comfort for them in their dealings with mathematics today and in their future.

▧ Evidence of Talent in Teaching

Brenda Hartshorn
Moretown, Vermont

My classroom would appear to a visitor to be a very busy, sometimes cluttered place, with children using a variety of materials as they discuss with each other what they are doing. I want my children to feel comfortable taking risks, to ask questions, and to explore many ways to solve a problem. Conversation fills the classroom throughout the day as children are engaged in project-based learning. Goals for my children include helping them develop the communication skills necessary to articulate what they know and how they came to know. In this way, we can have teacher-student dialogue about the problem-solving work they do. I can then create new instructional opportunities for the children on the basis of what they tell me and show me as I observe them at work.

My children also need a variety of problem-solving strategies modeled for them. There are times for direct instruction about strategies that can be used with certain mathematics problems. We try out many strategies for many problems. We discuss which ones are easier for some learners, and what other strategies are more efficient for other learners.

My children have been exposed to the characteristics of a good problem solver and have drawn pictures of times in their lives when they used these traits. Curiosity, persistence, flexibility, and reflection are the qualities we have focused on. Daily, I hear the children encouraging each other as they use these terms. One child said to another, "You are working hard. You are being persistent. I bet you feel good about the hard work you are doing." I am still trying to find ways to develop problem-solving skills for all my children as they are involved with meaningful mathematics situations.

I want all my children to use a wide variety of manipulatives when solving mathematics situations. They need some direct instruction to see the possibilities, and then they need to be given a choice of materials to use when they attempt to solve a problem. The materials I use in my classroom range from very simple household items like beans, dice, and playing cards to the more sophisticated school supplies like base-10 blocks, Cuisenaire rods, and pentominoes. Calculators, compasses, and rulers are used in answering questions the children come up with as they are learning through themes. Our recent ocean study led the children to discover the sizes of baby whales and the speed at which the babies travel with their mothers.

I want my children to be able to perform computations accurately just as much as I want them to find innovative ways to solve a familiar problem. We create many games with the manipulatives for practicing calculation "tricks." I hope my children are having a good time while they are learning about our number system. It is so important that they develop a strong sense of number concept so that complex mathematics situations may be explored with success and understanding.

I want my children to know about other maths. Geometry is a big part of my mathematics program. The children and I explore spatial problem solving by using pentominoes and tangrams. We build three-dimensional models by using compasses and straight edges. We learn how to draw three-dimensional pictures of dice structures by using isometric paper.

One of the most exciting units I have done with my children is a quilting unit. This study integrated children's literature, family and community connections, and many mathematics concepts. The more we got into this study, the more we discovered connections with numbers and geometry. I put together many of the ideas, but I stumbled across a wonderful resource—*Math Excursions* by Burk, Snider, and Symonds. I used some of their activities, although I had to adapt some of them to fit the age-group of my children.

Mathematical concepts we addressed were symmetry, rotation, tessellations, balance, color, shape, geometric relations, fractional parts ($1/2$ and $1/4$), measurement, and patterns. We used paper cut into different-size squares and triangles for most of our activities. The children also needed to do a lot of folding, cutting, rotating, and gluing.

One activity involved using four equal squares. Only two complimentary colors were used, the same for all the children. Two squares of each color and a white square of four times the size of each of the colored squares was used as a mat for gluing on the four small squares. Each child was to find all the ways these squares could be arranged on the white mat. Once these were shared and we were sure there were no other ways, we decided as a whole group which way to choose.

We glued our four squares onto the white mat in the same way. These were then called blocks and were used to create a paper quilt in three different patterns. They were also used to teach many ways to write and show the fraction $1/2$. If one block is used, then $1/2$ is $2/4$; if two blocks are used, then $1/2$ is $4/8$. One child noticed early on that the "bottom numbers were always the top numbers doubled."

Another activity presented the children with a picture of a quilt block and asked, "How many ways can you color this square so that $1/2$ is shaded?" Some children drew the picture over and over and colored them in random order. Other children used white paper mats to color in and compared their collections with a classmate's collection. Some children used paper cutouts to move around like puzzle pieces and then colored in a picture for each new way discovered. No one has solved the problem yet with a definite answer. It was more complicated than we thought at first and was a fun challenge for some children.

The children also needed to fold and cut squares to create triangles for creating specific quilt blocks. They also learned how to fold a large white paper mat to find the exact center. This folded mat was used to create a whole-class "Around the World Quilt" using "Where's Waldo?" wrapping paper and four colors of construction paper cut into 2-inch squares. This required a lot of concentration and cooperation as each group was responsible for a large block to be added to the completed paper quilt. All the blocks needed to be exactly alike for the pattern to occur.

The children chose fabric colors for a "real" quilt they helped make as a surprise for their student teacher. They had to help figure out the measurements of the finished quilt (what size would fit on her bed), the amount of fabric to buy, and the cost of the materials. The children helped cut the pieces; a paraeducator and I did the sewing on a machine in the classroom.

As a follow-up to our quilting unit, the class read *The Canada Geese Quilt,* by Natalie Kinsey Warnock, a Vermont author and quilt designer. I was able to get in touch with her, and she visited us with 10 quilts she designed and helped her grandmother sew. She also brought books she is writing that are in various stages. She told the children the stories that went with each quilt, the shapes and patterns she used, and how she worked out measurements.

Because I work with young children, the more tactile experiences I can provide for them, the better the chance of them making connections to their lives. The more real I can make their learning environment, the deeper their understandings will become. I am always trying to create a classroom that is stimulating, connected, and well-equipped with materials that allow children to become independent, successful learners.

I use a learning-styles inventory with my children to help give me more information about each child's strengths. I share this information with each child's parents, and we discuss ways to enhance the child's talents in the classroom. As a follow-up, I write to each child's parents in a home-school journal each week. We discuss their child's progress, areas that need new or renewed focus, and other information that can help us work as a team for creating a supportive, appropriate learning environment specific to the needs assessed.

When assessing children's mathematical understanding, I try to balance my time between asking questions of my children and standing back to observe what is being revealed to me through their work. I keep a journal that provides each child with a block of pages for observation notes. The children are given mathematics problems to solve that are connected to our themes. The problems are typed and provide lots of space for the children to draw and write their solutions and steps along the way.

I use these mathematics problem sheets to document our conversations about how they solved the problem, whether they were able to solve it another way, and what their level of understanding was of certain mathematics concepts. The children's drawings and writings are used to show parents where their children are mathematically and where I think we should lead them next. Observations and conversations with the children direct my planning for the next day for each child.

The Vermont Portfolio Math Criteria are used to assess my first-and second-grade students' mathematics work and problem-solving endeavors. I look for evidence of the criteria to assess my mathematics program. I want to make sure I am helping prepare my children for their portfolio challenges as fourth graders. The portfolio criteria provide me with a way to evaluate the types of activities I provide and the opportunities my children are given. I ask myself questions like, Do my students have a chance to use mathematical language frequently? Are they using mathematics representation in a variety of ways? and Are their strategies efficient and appropriate for the task at hand?

At times, I must change the approach I am using or the manipulative being used because a child demonstrates a need for something else or something more. At times, I need to ask another professional in the school to help me develop a new technique or to provide me with new ideas to use with a child having difficulties. This support network at my school keeps me growing as a professional. The staff at my school are talented and eager to work as a team. They provide me with great support and a rich environment for every child in our school.

Experiencing Sets of Numbers

Cindy Montonaro
Brunswick, Ohio

The following activity leads to much decision making and teamwork. To experience sets of numbers, I ask the children to stand by themselves in the middle of our classroom. I call a number, and the children gather themselves to form circles corresponding to that number. For example, I call the number 5, and the children anxiously go about the room trying to form circles of 5 students. When the correct number set is formed, those children hold hands and sit down on the floor, designating the set is completed. With 25 pupils, 5 sets will be made.

With certain numbers, some children may not be in a set. That's fine. They just stand over to the side of the other children. We then count the number of sets and the remainders (the children on the side who are not in a set). For example, 23 pupils will make 4 sets with 5 children in each, and 3 children will be left standing. If I call the number 7, then the children should make 3 sets of 7 and have 2 left as the remainder.

The decision making comes in when the children are trying to form the number set I called. Sometimes they need one or two more children for a set, so they call out to the other children for what they need. If one child is by herself, she then goes to join the group. Sometimes too many are in a set, and decisions are discussed and the children then discover what needs to be done to have the correct number set. This activity tends to have much excitement. The academic value, however, is immeasurable.

Creating an Elementary Mathematics Lending Library
Diane McCarty
Cedar Falls, Iowa

What do *Olympic Math; Theodoric's Rainbow; How Many Feet in the Bed?; Kids Make Pizza; Shake, Rattle, and Roll;* and *Benny's Pennies* have in common? They are all recently acquired books that are a part of the Price Laboratory Elementary School Mathematics Lending Library, which was initiated in the autumn of 1997. Let me tell you about this project.

In the spring of 1996, I received a $5,000 grant from the Carver Excellence in Education Teachers' Program for the development of a mathematics lending library for nursery/kindergarten through the fifth grade. The purpose of the lending library was to provide a way for parents and students to read good literature together at home and to explore varying concepts of mathematics with hands-on objects.

When the National Council of Teachers of Mathematics (NCTM) implemented new standards in 1988, a small revolution began in the way teachers were teaching mathematics. Some traditional methods that only emphasized algorithms and practice were being reshaped. More emphasis was being placed on students' understanding of mathematics and being able to communicate mathematically versus simply acquiring the "right" answers. Students began using problems within the constructs of their everyday lives and from the pages of good literature that took them into the world of problem solving well beyond a textbook-only program.

Throughout Iowa, as in many other states, teachers use appropriate literature, often in a thematic approach, to teach and enhance mathematical concepts. Manipulatives are being used into the intermediate grades and above so that concepts transfer more naturally into meaning for students. These serve as new and exciting ways for students to visualize mathematics; besides, it's fun! The only problem is that parents have often been left out of the loop in the change process in the teaching of mathematics. Families do not see the nightly mathematics homework that might have existed in the traditional program because much of the work is done in cooperative groups with hands-on learning. This type of learning is not always easy to demonstrate to parents, but the Price Laboratory School Mathematics Lending Library is an attempt to bridge that gap.

The Price Laboratory School (PLS) elementary teachers worked throughout the 1996-97 school year, researching, reading, and investigating ideas for implementing such a library. In the spring of 1997, the elementary teachers purchased their literature selections for each classroom and then found appropriate materials to add to these books for family enjoyment. (We even went on a faculty field trip to two bookstores one Saturday!)

More than 25 titles for each classroom have been sent home individually on a rotating basis since this project was kicked off at our fall Open House. Games, recipes, play coins and paper money, timing devices, dominoes, cards, dice, and counting pieces (e.g., plastic elephants or ants) are a few of the many manipulatives that have been bagged with these books and become a part of the send-home packages. Families have discovered books that pose problems to be solved, problems to be created, items to be manipulated, pictures to be drawn, shapes to be cut, fun times, and mathematical thinking taking place as they collaboratively enjoy their lending library kits.

Our faculty is connecting home with our existing program, which closely uses the NCTM Standards, manipulative usage to teach mathematics concepts, and children's literature in an integrated curriculum. Now parents can see the value in such a program through activities that are included in the take-home kits.

The PLS Mathematics Lending Library—Connecting Home has been functioning for almost 1 full school year now. The families' journal entries are showing that some tremendous mathematical connections are being made. One journal entry drawn by a fourth grader shows fractional parts of a pizza being eaten by individual members at their house. The pizza had been made from a recipe in the book *Kids Making Pizza* kit, which was complete with a pizza pan, measuring spoons, and cups in this particular hanging bag. Another child took an instant picture of the rainbow created in his house with a prism that was part of the kit containing the book *Theodoric's Rainbow.*

Each week, students in my classroom have informally reported insights about the kits as they are checked in with all items accounted for before they are rotated to a new student for another week. Here is a sampling of the comments I have documented from the students:

I had *Test Your Number Power* last week. The one I recommend in that book is Nimble Numbers. It is really challenging. I bet I tried a ton of ways to solve that one, but I just couldn't get it. I didn't really want to look at the answer either. After about an hour, though, I looked it up and then figured out how it was supposed to be done.

The Allowance Game taught me that money is not made out of thin air.

I like the *Shake, Rattle, and Roll* math book. The game format was fun for me and my family.

Arithmetic (by Carl Sandburg) was really cool. The Mylar sheet was fun, and I'd like to try it around a soda can. That would be cool.

Calculator Mania was really fun, but I also see how I was learning at the same time.

It has been an exciting year to pilot the PLS Mathematics Lending Library. On numerous occasions, faculty members have shared with me the connections or extensions that students have made from a home mathematical activity to a school mathematical activity. As the end of the year approaches, the faculty will gather survey data from parents and students, assess the data, and decide how we can better reconnect home with our mathematics lending library in the future. This project resulted in a mathematical bonding experience for all.

Helpful Tips

1. *Go slowly.* Take time to find good mathematics-related literature and supporting activities that will be enticing and fun for families to enjoy together.

2. *Start small.* Begin with a few titles, manipulatives, or suggested related activities for just your classroom. The library can always grow to other levels as money and means become available.

3. *Be creative.* Find mathematics everywhere and let your literature selections and your suggested activities reflect this thought. An atlas has a lot of mathematics, as do science experiments, hopscotch, and magic tricks. Do not limit your ideas; true mathematical connections abound all around us.

4. *Have fun.* Be sold on your lending library concept and implement it wisely, and it will be successful with students and parents. Involve as many people as you can to spread the workload and increase the opportunities for positive collaborations within your school.

"Mathville, Mississippi"

Edna M. Waller
Ocean Springs, Mississippi

During the past few years, I have been working to implement more of an application approach to the mathematics curriculum for my students at Magnolia Park Elementary School. Even though they were mastering the basic skills, they did not seem to understand the practical application of mathematics. Modern business and industry leaders have also voiced a concern that graduates of the public school system are not adept at practical, everyday mathematical problem solving. Critical-thinking skills are often lost or not expanded as students strive to master basic isolated skills.

I wanted to develop a unit that would not only enhance the basic skills of addition, multiplication, division, and subtraction but also show students the use of these and other mathematical skills in the world around them. I wanted my students to study how mathematics was used in various careers and professions and to establish a connection between problem solving and real-life situations. This was also to be a unit of study that would lend itself to an integrated curriculum approach in which students could focus on their talents and interests.

During a previous project, my students and I had worked with students in a self-contained classroom for the learning disabled. It was such a rewarding experience for us that I wanted to include these students in the new project. I discussed this possibility with Mrs. Cindy Johnson, one of our special education teachers. We decided to bring her students, once a week during their mathematics time, in with my class to work on a unit in practical mathematical applications. "Mathville, Mississippi," as we named it, involved the students in the study of various careers and occupations and the use of mathematics in solving problems related to those careers and occupations. Working together, students planned, constructed, and operated stores, businesses, and agencies by using necessary mathematics, social, and creative skills. They worked as cashiers, bank tellers, waitpersons, shop owners, and travel agents and in doing so solved a great variety of mathematical problems.

"Mathville, Mississippi" was a year-long project that began in September with the students researching the practical application of mathematics in specific jobs, careers, and professions. The students were eager to select the jobs and types of businesses they wanted to operate. After some discussion on how they would choose, they decided to create a list by brainstorming different occupations and businesses. Then each student chose a job and wrote a short paragraph describing the duties of that particular job. We ran into a problem when more than one person wanted the same job, but the students decided to be democratic and draw names when necessary.

During the first week in November, the students began shopping for supplies for their businesses from the wholesalers (Mrs. Johnson and me). Supplies included stationery products, art supplies, snacks for the restaurant, candies, prescriptions for the drugstore, toys, and so on. Parents donated most of these supplies. Each student had to decide how much he or she could afford to spend and what the business needed each day. I introduced calculator skills to the younger students and reinforced these skills with the older students. In this era of modern technology, it is very important for students to learn to use all the electronic tools available to them. This was a wonderful reinforcement for the basic skills they were learning in mathematics.

During the second week of the simulation, the students received ledger sheets to complete. They counted their money at the beginning of each Mathville day and placed these amounts in the proper place on their ledger sheets. The students recorded the income and payments they had to balance at the end of each day. During the third week, the students received receipt books to record all sales. We reviewed addition, subtraction, and multiplication as necessary. Fate cards of natural disasters, medical emergencies, and bonuses were drawn daily. Mathville, Mississippi, was a very active place, and mathematics skills were in constant use.

The simulation of running an actual business continued through April, during mathematics time 1 or 2 days a week. As mayor of Mathville, I held daily conferences with the students and worked with them individually on problems that arose. Keeping the ledger sheets straight was difficult for them at first, and they rarely balanced out at the end of the day. Someone usually forgot to write a receipt or to save a receipt, and this made it difficult to keep accurate records. As the simulation progressed, however, the students began to see the importance of keeping track of their sales and their spending. They were very excited when they ended the day with the right amount of money.

About halfway through the simulation, the students and I began preparing for the exhibit that would bring over more than 600 students through Mathville, Mississippi. During the following days, using their measuring and creative skills, they designed and constructed buildings from 4 × 8-foot sheets of plywood. During one session, the students were having a difficult time keeping their lines straight. This led to a discussion on parallel lines and what tools and skills they needed to make sure the lines were straight. The students were then able to complete their designs. This was one of many opportunities for short mathematics lessons within the larger project.

During the next few weeks, the students painted their buildings and made a sign for each. They wrote short presentations on the particular occupations they had chosen. These included a physician, pharmacist, zookeeper, banker, postmaster, recreation worker, nurse, newspaper editor, restaurant manager, waitress, and florist. Each student gave background information on his or her chosen profession. Educational requirements, job opportunities, salaries, and the use of mathematics in these professions were included. The students reinforced writing skills, as well as research skills, during this time.

The students also formulated mathematical problems that persons in their occupations might encounter. Because the students who would be visiting Mathville ranged in grade level from kindergarten to fifth grade, the students had to create mathematics problems of various levels of difficulty to present to the visitors. After writing their presentations, the students practiced giving them orally. Skills in verbal presentation and speech were reinforced.

The students also made various products to sell to the visitors. They designed stationery, bookmarks, note cards, buttons, and postcards. We also solicited items from businesses and parents. We purchased items as well with money we received through a grant with Mississippi Power. As the buildings were finished, the students created posters describing the use of mathematics in each profession and placed them in each business. Some students designed logos for Mathville and created an invitation for the exhibit. A final edition of the *Mathville Press* was published with short excerpts from the evaluations the students had written about their experiences in Mathville, Mississippi.

During the week of the exhibit, students from the regular education classrooms came with their teachers to visit Mathville. Each student was given $10.00 of Mathville money to spend in any stores of his or her choosing. A brief presentation by the Mathville students on their various careers and occupations gave the visitors some information before they shopped. The shopowners and other professionals (students) wrote receipts, calculated change, and answered any questions the visitors had.

During the following weeks, the students heard from resource persons from the community on various occupations and how they use mathematics in these occupations. Some of these individuals were parents of the students, and some were volunteers from the local community. The students also completed independent studies on careers of their choosing. They constructed graphs of their sales over the course of the simulation and also filled out their income tax forms and calculated their income tax.

"Mathville, Mississippi" certainly taught my students a lot about mathematics. They also learned a great deal of practical application of mathematics in the workplace. Their problem-solving and reasoning skills increased, and they exhibited a great deal of creativity. Perhaps one of the most valuable lessons they learned was how to work with each other in a meaningful and productive way. If you were to ask the students, however, they would tell you that the best part of "Mathville, Mississippi" was the fun.

Engaging and Purposeful Math

Kathi Orr
Moretown, Vermont

When I first started teaching in 1980, I used a textbook for each of my first and second graders. They did workbook pages each day for "math time." I now regret that I taught this way. As I grew more confident in my teaching ability, I decided that I did not need a textbook for each child or myself anymore. We never finished all 342 pages anyway. A lot seemed to be missing from my mathematics program. I thought the children needed to use mathematics in purposeful and exciting ways. They needed to become excited about what they were exploring and discovering, rather than about what page they were on compared with their classmates. They needed to see firsthand that there can be several different ways to solve a mathematics problem. I knew what the main units were in the mathematics curriculum, so I devised my own lesson plans and generated my own materials to teach the concepts and skills.

As I undertook this change in my teaching style, I became one of Rachel McAnallen's students. Her hands-on approach using manipulatives for every unit generating number sense excited me and affirmed my conviction that my new teaching style was going in the right direction. I wanted to share my excitement with my children. As I became a lifelong learner and modeled mathematical behavior, it was absorbed by my children. They frequently said, "Can we do math?" or "Is this math?" Many of them became upset if they thought we had missed math during the day.

Each year, I used budget money I would have used to purchase textbooks to purchase new manipulatives for my children. As a result, my classroom is filled with manipulatives such as hundreds, tens, and ones blocks; tangrams; Geoboards; compasses; straight edges; dice; and an overhead projector.

Rachel's influence stayed with me as I branched out to enhance my mathematics program by adding a literature component to the manipulatives in my classroom. Mathematics literature in my classroom library allows my children to see that mathematics is everywhere. The titles I have include *Pigs Will Be Pigs* (money connection), *The Greedy Triangle* (geometry), *Smart* by Shel Silverstein (money), *The Emperor's New Cloak* (geometry), and *Alexander Used to Be Rich on Sunday* (money). The many journeys we take on finding answers to questions influenced by the literature lead us to become persistent, flexible, curious, and reflective. Listening to and observing the children justifying their reasoning is inspirational.

I have also found computer programs that integrate and support my mathematics program. I often preview programs to make sure my software library contains more than drill and practice. Two programs that are a favorite with my children are Tesselmania, by MECC, and Discover Time, by Sunburst.

In recent years, the NCTM Standards, Marilyn Burns, and the Vermont Portfolio Math Criteria have kept my enthusiasm burning. I have found that the ideas generated by each integrates easily with the manipulatives, literature, and problem solving I am doing in my classroom.

Marilyn Burns has been a major influence as I develop problems to integrate with mathematics units I teach. She, along with my children, have caused me always to consider the following: (a) How does the problem reflect my values and beliefs about children and learning mathematics? (b) Is the problem engaging and purposeful to my children? and (c) What do I want to assess (e.g., strategies, cooperative learning skills, mathematics facts)?

Money is one of my favorite mathematics units. One problem I pose to my children to figure out is this: I have 3 coins in my pocket; how much money could I have? The children were very curious to find out what the coins were and the highest amount of money it was possible for me to have in my pocket. They were so engaged as they shared their ideas with others. Some children even shared the problem with their parents at home and brought in additional possibilities.

We even estimated how many combinations we could come up with. Some children asked questions such as, "Could one coin be a silver dollar?" "Could they all be the same kind of coin?" "Do they all have smooth edges or rough edges?" and "How many have smooth edges, and how many have rough edges?" These questions are evidence of good thinking, applying skills/knowledge they have gained, and working on a problem with a purpose. I was able to watch and listen to see how well they could identify coins and their values. I watched to see how well they could count money.

I could assess their counting skills by 1s, 5s, 10s, or 25s as they were actively engaged in solving the problem. I could hear and see them speaking and writing mathematics language. I saw them plan their strategies and justify their answers. Their "writings" or dictations to explain their thought processes in this coin problem became pieces in their mathematics portfolios.

We chant a song (by Rachel McAnallen) frequently throughout the days/weeks:

Five pennies trade a nickel, two nickels trade a dime, two nickels and a dime trade a quarter every time. Four quarters trade a dollar and that is quite a lot, and a dollar is exactly how much I have got!

We also get a penny for each day we are in school. This helps reinforce coin recognition, value, trading, and counting money on a daily basis even though money is not always the unit we are working on.

I ask parents to send in real money from home when we work on money for an intense period of time. I believe that children understand money and its concepts better if they use the real things. Thus, each child has a bank made from an egg carton with four sections: penny, nickel, dime, and quarter. With the bank, each child has a wallet. A wallet is divided into five sections: penny, nickel, dime, quarter, dollar. We roll a hexahedron (die) to see how many pennies we can put into our wallets. When a child gets five or more pennies, he can say our trade and put five pennies into the bank and take out a nickel to put into his wallet. Trading continues until a dollar is reached.

Many variations, such as paying taxes (subtracting money from their wallets) and receiving bonuses at work, are added to this basic game to practice addition and subtraction. The basic money-trading game directions and its variations, along with wallets, are sent home with the children so that they can "teach" their moms and dads about money.

Another activity we do is a coin timeline. We look at the year on our coins and order them from oldest to newest. In addition, we classify and graph coins according to their attributes, such as smooth edges, rough edges, and color.

I read the class literature that focuses on money. In many cases, we have a problem to figure out after or during the reading of the story. For example, in the book *Pigs Will Be Pigs,* each member of the pig family finds money in a different spot around the home. The children are asked to find out how much money the family has in all. When the pigs go out to eat, the children are asked to find out how much money the pig family will have to pay for their meals. Last, the children find out whether the pigs have any money left over. After much cooperation, flexibility, persistence, and reflection while trying various strategies, we come up with answers all of us agree on in this case. As a follow-up project, we can write our own big book version or rewrite of this story.

Another literature piece I use with my money unit is *The Gingerbread Man.* On reading the story, the children are able to make and decorate a gingerbread person. Each item has a price indicated (e.g., gumdrops 5 cents each, raisins 10 cents each). Each child has to tell me how much his or her gingerbread person would cost after making a table listing items used, quantity of each item, price of each item, and the total prices.

In short, money, as with most mathematics units, is ongoing. It does not just fill a few weeks of time. Mathematics is all around us all the time. The children's faces beam as they realize they have just used their mathematical skills without realizing it. Their confidence as mathematicians and problems solvers must be nurtured and celebrated.

▨ Touching the Sky: Kites in the Classroom
Nancy Ann Belsky
Westmoreland, New Hampshire

Kites and kids! What a great combination. Kites, which have been made and flown for thousands of years, are a link to the imagination of our students. Through the years, I have found some kites that really fly that can be made inexpensively in the classroom. Constructing the kites provides a practical application for many of the mathematics skills I teach my students during the year.

Students also learn to follow written and illustrated directions. I pair or put the students in groups of two to four. Each group is given written instructions I expect its members to follow to make a full-size pattern for the kite. Once I check the patterns and discuss them with each group, the groups construct their kites. They must carefully plan the correct size of the finished kites, taking into account the materials available. To complete their kites successfully, they must work cooperatively, use ratios to enlarge the pattern to fit the dimensions of the finished products, and measure, cut, and construct them.

The materials you use for the kites must be light and strong. Keeping the kites within a school budget is also a concern, so these materials are inexpensive or readily available in a school setting. The sail of a kite can be made from paper (tissue, newsprint, or roll paper) or plastic trash bags. I have found that paper is easier to handle but that plastic holds up better in the sky. Spars can be made from drinking straws for quite small kites or dowels ranging in diameter from $\frac{1}{8}$ inch to $\frac{1}{4}$ inch; these can be purchased in hardware and hobby stores.

Tails or streamers, which are used to balance the kite, also add style and individuality. Crepe paper streamers, strips cut from plastic bags, surveyor's tape, and a variety of ribbons can all be used for tails. Let the students be creative, but be sure the tail is light enough for the kite and doesn't drag it down.

The string used to fly a kite must fit the kite. For very light kites that won't go far, crochet or button thread is ideal. Kite or household string usually works best. Don't use fish twine; it can be dangerous and, when tangled in trees, becomes a hazard for birds. I provide string for half the number of students in the class and expect them to work cooperatively and take turns launching their kites. That avoids too many kites in the air at once, limiting the number of tangled lines.

When you are ready to fly the kites, it is handy to have a few extra adults. Bring with you a "kite first-aid kit" consisting of tape, extra streamers, extra dowels, string, and scissors. Be sure the scissors stay in your or another responsible adult's possession.

To make sure everyone stays safe, review these rules with your class before you fly the kites:

- Fly your kite in open spaces that are flat and unobstructed.

- Do not fly a kite in stormy or rainy weather.

- Do not fly your kite over people. A falling kite is dangerous.

- Do not fly your kite near power lines. If a kite does land on a power line, LEAVE IT THERE. Notify the local utility company. DO NOT TRY TO TAKE IT DOWN YOURSELF! Don't even tug on the string.

- To avoid cut hands, wear gloves when flying a strong-pulling kite.

- Do not fly kites near airfields or in airplane traffic patterns. Kites have caused airplane accidents.

- Watch out for birds when flying kites. Strings can cut them. Flying kites can also disturb nesting birds.

Many kinds of kites are easy to make and fly well. I have found that sled kites are the easiest to make and are almost foolproof flyers in light or moderate wind; they are great for beginners of any age from kindergarten through college. Deltas are easily flown but a bit more complex to make. Tetrahedrons are flashy and look great hanging in the classroom; they fly well but are easily broken when they fall. The fine-motor skills needed to tie the knots make third or fourth grade the lower limit for constructing tetrahedrons. Box kites are sophisticated kites for experienced flyers; they are more appropriate for middle schoolers. Libraries and bookstores have great books about kite making and flying.

Watching students fly their kites is fascinating. Young students equate flying kites with physical movement. They love the activity of running with their kites flying behind them; they don't have the patience to stand and play out the line. As the students reach middle school, they begin to try to see how high up they can get their kites. For many students, your class may be the first successful experience they have had with this exciting hobby. After a unit on kites, I can tell my students to touch the sky and I know they can.

CHAPTER **4**

Exploring Science, Mathematics, and Technology

*H*ow are your colleagues exploring mathematics, science, and technology?

Chapter Overview

- **Judith Olson**, an instructional services consultant at Lakeland Area Agency 3 in Cylinder, Iowa, shares an interdisciplinary curriculum model with an aviation education theme.

- **Juliann Bliese**, a K-1 teacher at O'Loughlin Elementary School in Hays, Kansas, explains "Goat Bridges," a science activity in which students are challenged to build a bridge that can hold weight.

- **Nancy E. Baker**, a first-grade teacher at Petersburg Elementary School in Pageland, South Carolina, provides the steps necessary to make "Icky Sticky Gloop." She discusses science considerations and activity-based learning.

- **M. Katheryn Grimes**, a science specialist at the Gwendolyn Woolley Elementary School in Las Vegas, Nevada, explains Project S.M.I.L.E., which is "a program for at risk fifth grade students at Woolley Elementary School in northern Las Vegas, Nevada."

➡ **Sandra Miller** is a fourth-grade teacher at North Star Elementary School in Nikiski, Alaska. Her class is linked with the National Weather Service in Anchorage and is an official weather observation site.

➡ **Shirley J. Wright**, a gifted/talented facilitator at Gate City Elementary School in Pocatello, Idaho, is deeply concerned about the pressing need and impetus for school reform, especially in the areas of science and mathematics.

➡ **Elvira Bitsoi Largie**, a teacher/administrative intern at Newcomb Middle School in Newcomb, New Mexico, discusses the importance of culturally relevant curricula.

Interdisciplinary Curriculum Model: Aviation Education

Judith Olson
Cylinder, Iowa

TITLE: We're Taking One Small Step Into First Grade, One Giant Leap Into Learning

PURPOSE: To provide an excitement to learn in our orbiter called *Discovery*. Our mission is first grade. Mrs. Olson is the commander; our leader is the pilot each day; and the girls and boys in our classroom are the mission specialists.

LEARNING OBJECTIVES: Standards and Benchmarks

1. Understands the basic features of Earth
   – Knows that weather changes from day to day but that things like temperature (or snow) tend to be high, low, or medium in the same months every year

2. Understands motion and the principles that explain it
   – Knows that an object's motion can be changed by a push or a pull by people or by other objects

3. Understands the essential concepts about nutrition and diet
   – Classifies food and food combinations according to the food groups

4. Understands that, in science, it is helpful to work with a team and share findings with others
   - Contributes to the overall effort of a group
   - Demonstrates leadership skills
   - Maintains a healthy self-concept
   - Explores career possibilities, resource speakers, field trips

VOCABULARY:

mission, hypothesis, parachute, teamwork, space shuttle, experiment, scientist, external tank, free fall, gravity, orbiter, zero gravity, engineer, solid rocket boosters, launch window, motion, weather, precipitation, water cycle, leadership, problem solving, careers, goals, exploration

INTEGRATION WITH OTHER SUBJECTS:

Literacy—journals, pilot reflections each day, literature connections

Science Connections—investigations and experiments using scientific method, flight connections, kite making and flying, GLOBE Weather Project (taking measurements and entering data on the Internet)

Careers—famous Americans (each child portrays a famous American with a report and costume)

Social Action—100 day activities, grocery store activity handing out healthful foods and explaining food pyramid

Technology Connections—Internet, word processing, CD-ROMs, digital camera imagery

Leadership Development—pilot of the day (leadership and teamwork)

Research—learn steps of a quality research paper, sources of information (bibliography), presentation skills

Mathematics—estimation, investigations involving measurement, mathematics journals, mathematics careers, student surveys, graphing activities, probability, and statistics

Parental Involvement—parent volunteers, parent resources

Constructivist Approach to Developmentally Appropriate Programs

In our first grade, most of our learning is hands-on exploration activities. We use the constructivist approach to learning, building on prior learning. We do many activities to make the children aware of gravity, Newton's laws of motion, proper nutrition, and career awareness. Parental involvement is an important connection to the whole learning process. We hold parent-teacher conferences during the first week of school, at the end of the first 9 weeks, and between the second and third 9 weeks.

Parents volunteer to work with the children on a daily or weekly basis at our school, or on field trips, or during demonstrations and presentations in our community. It is important to empower parents in their children's journey through learning and life. Reflections by children and their parents are important in the learning process: "We learn by doing, if we reflect on what we have done" (John Dewey).

Remember, if children are challenged and involved, discipline problems are few. We need to understand the multiple intelligences and gifts of all children so that we can see their excitement and passion for learning. Our children are living postcards that we are preparing for a period of time that we may never see. We must prepare them for that time.

Goat Bridges

Juliann Bliese
Hays, Kansas

The activity "Goat Bridges" is integrated with the story *Three Billy Goats Gruff*. The children transform potatoes into goats by using toothpicks for legs and decorations. They work in groups of three to construct their bridges for the three billy goats. The goal of this learning experience is to construct a bridge that can hold weight. The criterion is to build the bridge so that it is at least 5 inches off the ground and at least 24 inches long.

Target skills include observing likenesses and differences; planning; experimenting; comparing length, width, and height; measuring holding capacity; working together as a team to make decisions on a project that result in one sample; recording data; and explaining group projects through oral team reports.

The bridge must be strong enough to hold a large potato goat. The largest potato weighed approximately 1 pound. Before the children could begin, they worked together to select "junk" materials for their bridges from the junk pile. They also drew bridge plans, and members of each group had to agree on its plan. I checked, discussed, and approved the plans before the actual building began.

This project takes several days to complete. The children went all out and constructed bridges that went above and beyond the requirements. Emerging leaders in groups were of both genders. I learned a lot about the individual children in my room as I watched the dynamics of this project unfold. This activity integrated language arts, story sequencing, story retelling, comprehension, generalization, and dramatics, along with mathematics, science, and social skills.

Helpful Tips

I favor inquiry-based, hands-on learning. I do not give set answers or expect uniform answers from the children, but rather "discovery" based on what my children experience. I ask many questions, not always expecting an answer, but rather encouraging the children to think of alternatives. I want my children to be risk takers, to try various methods and alternatives, to learn that failure is OK. Failure (something not working) within an activity is just part of the activity and a learning experience.

I promote movement. I cannot sit still myself and do not expect my children to learn sitting in one spot for an extended period of time. Science is exciting, invigorating, and moving. I promote discussion of alternative ideas. I want to know why my children think the way they do. I integrate science with the overall central learning theme present in the classroom.

Science learning complements and reinforces learning goals in all areas of the curriculum. It permeates through our stories, poems, mathematics centers, singing, research projects, art, social studies, computer multimedia projects, lunchtime, recess, and our everyday world. It is not just one part of the day; it is part of everything we do in our classroom all day long. I do not use science dittos or worksheets. The recording we do is in our journals, on teacher-child-made graphs, or on charts.

I always begin a new unit of science with a KWL (What We *K*now, What We *W*ant to Know, and What We *L*earned) Chart. It allows me to find out what my children already know about a specific concept. It also allows the children to help set the path of their own learning with questions they want to explore. I add these questions in with my own predetermined goals and objectives to make learning meaningful and motivating to my children. As the unit unfolds, we check back to the chart, answering some questions and documenting what we learned. We also add new questions as we answer old ones. Science is a constant, moving, ever-learning journey to explore.

The children are an integral part of the science learning plan as they help develop the learning scope with their previous knowledge and questions for further learning. I view science as an exciting, moving, experimenting, questioning force in our daily lives.

Icky Sticky Gloop and Inquiry Science

Nancy E. Baker
Pageland, South Carolina

OBJECTIVES:

1. The children will explore properties—states of matter (liquids and solids).

2. The children will observe changes in states of matter.

3. The children will develop basic process skills.

FRAMEWORK CORRELATION:

Area III: Matter and Energy

Strand 3: Changes in Matter

Pre K-3 Standard: The children should know and be able to recognize that matter can be changed in form (solids, liquids, and gases).

PROCESSES INVOLVED:

Observing, predicting, inferring, classifying, and communicating

MATERIALS NEEDED:

White glue (2 parts)

Liquid starch (1 part)

Paper cups or other small containers (3-oz)

Large cups (10-oz)

Craft sticks

BACKGROUND INFORMATION:

Icky Sticky Gloop is a mixture of white glue and liquid starch. It consists of 2 parts glue to 1 part liquid starch. It is assumed before this lesson that the child has considerable experiences with the states of matter and can define the properties of solids and the properties of liquids.

PREPARATION:

The children should work in pairs. Provide each child with three (3-oz) containers marked 1, 2, and 3. Two of the containers should hold glue; one should hold liquid starch. Do not tell the children the contents of the containers. If the instructor wants to include quantitative observations, the children can measure the amounts of the liquids, as well as the mass of the finished Gloop. Each child should also have a large container and a craft stick. An activity sheet is attached for the children's use if the instructor wishes to do so.

ENGAGEMENT PHASE:

Read to the class the book *Icky Sticky Gloop* (by Morgan Matthews). Talk with the children about inventors. Tell them that today they are going to be inventors.

EXPLORATION PHASE:

1. Examine the contents of Container 1. Ask the following:
   – What is the color of the substance?

– How does it smell?

– What happens when you move the container around?

– How heavy is the substance? (Feel the weight of the container.)

– Touch the contents with your finger. How does it feel?

– What other observations can you make about this substance?

– What do you think Substance 1 is?

2. Examine the contents of Container 2.

   – Repeat the same questions you asked about Container 1.

3. Examine the contents of Container 3.

   – Repeat the same questions you asked about Container 1.

4. Predict what will happen when the contents of the three containers are mixed.

5. Pour the contents of the three small containers together into the large container. Mix with a craft stick for several minutes. When the mixture begins to pull away from the side of the container, remove the mixture from the container by hand. Knead it like dough until smooth. *Note:* If the mixture is stringy, add a little more glue; if it is sticky or runny, add more starch.

CONCEPT DEVELOPMENT PHASE:

Review with the children what happened during the exploration phase. Ask and discuss the following questions:

■ What are the states of matter?

■ What state were the substances in before they were mixed?

■ How do you know?

■ What state were they in after they were mixed together?

■ How do you know?

■ What are some differences between solids and liquids?

CONCEPT APPLICATION:

Discuss the following:

1. Name some liquids.

2. Name some solids.

3. Name other times a liquid can become a solid.

4. Name other times a solid may become a liquid.

5. Discuss possible reasons for these changes.

EXTENSIONS:

1. Allow the children to experiment with the Icky Sticky Gloop. It will pick up prints as Silly Putty does and will bounce. The children can blow bubbles with the Gloop by placing it on one end of a straw and blowing gently into the other end.

2. The children can design an advertisement for the sale of their newly invented product.

3. The children can explore safety factors in inventing.

4. The children can research famous inventors. (The main character in the book *Icky Sticky Gloop* is Benjamin Franklin Bunny.)

5. The children can explore fractional parts.

Science Considerations

Science process skills provide children with the tools to unlock the mystery of the world around them about which they have a genuine natural curiosity. Science concepts provide avenues for a totally integrated curriculum to emanate so that learning has validity and connections are made. For meaningful learning to occur, however, the child must be an active participant. True inquiry science requires a child to be involved in laboratory activities at least 50% of the instructional time. By actually experiencing science, interest is maintained and knowledge is internalized.

All inquiry lessons should follow the learning cycle format, which includes the following phases:

Engagement Phase: This phase provides the "hook" for the lesson. It may include the posing of a problem, a KWL (What We *K*now, What We *W*ant to Know, and What We *L*earned) Chart, or relating to previous lessons.

Exploration Phase: The child is provided with materials and guidelines. Time is given for the child to experiment and come to some understanding on her or his own.

Concept Development Phase: In this phase, the teacher brings together the lesson and, through questioning and discussion, develops the concepts of the lesson. Misunderstandings can also be eliminated during this phase.

Application Phase: In this phase, the child applies the concepts of the lesson to a new situation. Through the learning cycle approach, problem-solving skills and higher order thinking skills are promoted. Interest in learning is maintained, and enthusiasm for science is prevalent.

Activity-Based Learning

The goal of education should be to equip children with skills that will enable them to become adept at facilitating their own learning, thus creating lifelong learners. Using experiences that give children an understanding of science process skills provides them with strategies to engage successfully in all aspects of life. Authentic connections among curriculum areas weave the thread of realism into the classroom. Learning becomes purposeful and meaningful.

The program I designed for my children has caused my classroom to become a hub of activity and meaningful learning. Centered around science concepts and process skills that encourage problem solving and higher level thinking skills through the learning cycle approach, the program takes an integrated hands-on approach to education. The children are challenged on a whole-group, cooperative group, and individual basis. Expectations are high, and enthusiasm is fervent. My overall goal for the children is to feel successful and accomplished.

Helpful Tips

To meet the needs of my children, I carefully plan strategies and activities that address varied learning styles, as well as modalities. Cooperative groups are often formed on the basis of the group's learning styles, which I have formally identified, and each investigation contains visual, auditory, and kinesthetic components. The wide range of abilities in my classroom offers a wonderful opportunity for children of varying talents to share their knowledge and to learn from one another in cooperative groups. My children thrive with the knowledge that I consider them "coteachers."

I handle monitoring through constant interaction with my children and observation. Discussions following activities and science journals provide me with insight into their comprehension. Each major investigation is followed by at least one other activity in which the children must apply the knowledge they have absorbed in previous activities. Always the goal is to pursue a higher level of thinking.

Authentic instruction must be assessed by authentic assessment. Therefore, I use a variety of tools, including portfolios, projects (long-term, self-designed investigations), and unit tests. Teacher-student-made rubrics are used to evaluate portfolios and projects. One aspect of the portfolio is the completion of a concept map.

Extending our classroom beyond the walls by remaining in contact with parents is a vital aspect of my program. Parents volunteer time to the classroom, and we all provide ideas to extend the learning at home. When we all work together to ensure a meaningful, risk-free curriculum for the children, we have succeeded in enabling the children to accomplish whatever they choose to pursue in life.

Project S.M.I.L.E. (Science Museum and Instructional Laboratory for the Environment)

M. Katheryn Grimes
Las Vegas, Nevada

Project S.M.I.L.E. is a program for at-risk fifth-grade students at Woolley Elementary School in northern Las Vegas, Nevada. These students are identified by their classroom teachers as needing that "extra boost" academically and socially. Typically, students in Project S.M.I.L.E. are somewhat withdrawn and low in self-esteem. Instead of becoming the recipients of peer tutoring from more advanced students (traditional methods), these at-risk students themselves become academic leaders for visitors to the school campus.

Funded by generous federal, state, and local grants, Project S.M.I.L.E. consists of a natural history museum, science laboratory, and desert educational garden located at Woolley Elementary School. The museum houses fossils from the Paleozoic, Mesozoic, and Cenozoic Eras; a life-size model of the sabre-toothed tiger, which once roamed Nevada; rare minerals and artifacts from the mining industry in Nevada; memorabilia from the building of the Hoover Dam; a display of flora and fauna from the Las Vegas wetlands; and Native American (ancient and modern) artifacts.

The science laboratory houses a state-of-the-art technology center, 84-gallon aquariums, animal habitats, and extensive scientific equipment and supplies. Located outside the science laboratory is the large desert garden. Students identified for this program (approximately 50) choose their area of expertise from the museum, laboratory, or garden and research together information they would like to teach to other students. Under the theoretical framework "umbrella" of social constructivism, these S.M.I.L.E. teams meet once a week for 2 hours of study until they are ready to accept "tours" of visiting students to our school (usually about 2 months).

As visitors come to this program (once a week for 2 hours), S.M.I.L.E. members take over the teaching. They keep detailed journals of their feelings before, during, and after the tours. Feedback sessions are conducted during the lunchtime after each tour to discuss what went right and what went wrong that particular day. The sessions encourage team members. This "flip-flop," if you will, of having these students becoming successful academic experts is the opposite of traditional methods of remediation.

Qualitative research conducted on Project S.M.I.L.E. has shown an increase in these students' participation in their regular classrooms, school activities, family responsibilities, autonomy, and (most significantly) empowerment. Some quotes from student journals and conversations: "I felt great because they didn't know something I knew"; "I felt important, more important than I ever have before"; and "This is the best day of my life."

Project S.M.I.L.E. was established in 1991 and receives approximately 750 to 1,000 student visitors each school year. Many of these visiting students have written to the team members, saying how much they learned from them and how they loved being taught by another student. As I watch the interaction with S.M.I.L.E. team members and their guests, I truly see the concept of "community of learners" because these young people recognize and embrace diversity as they exchange knowledge with each other. This program has taught me to concentrate on dumping the "old school" attitude (that teachers are fountains of all knowledge). Rather, we have the charge to give students an opportunity to construct their knowledge socially, providing mentoring and guidance.

Helpful Tips

This type of project must have the total commitment of the school community—administrators, classroom teachers, students, their families, and even support staff. Pulling students out of class for 2 hours a week can cause problems for classroom teachers and some students. The extra effort it requires certainly pays off in the long run. Scheduling can be troublesome at times, however.

My philosophy of education has gone through a tremendous transformation because of S.M.I.L.E. students. We are no longer a part of the Industrial Revolution/Authoritarian Age, but a part of a postmodern society where team players work together to construct lifelong learning. Project S.M.I.L.E. taught me.

The National Weather Service Project: Real-Life Connections in the Classroom

Sandra Miller
Nikiski, Alaska

Finding ways to incorporate classroom learning with real-life situations is a focal point of my teaching. There is no doubt that students enjoy a greater degree of academic success when an area of study is directly tied to their family or community. This year, my class linked with the National Weather Service in Anchorage, Alaska, to become an official weather observation site. Funding made available from two minigrants allowed me to purchase an automated weather station, a classroom computer, and two global positioning systems.

This ongoing daily project has resulted in numerous exciting spin-offs, particularly in the areas of science and mathematics. The following explains the project and some activities that have resulted. Each day, between 12:30 p.m. and 2:30 p.m., a student team "dials up" the weather station via a modem connection in the classroom. Once the data are displayed, the team records the information. Three or four students then go outside, cloud chart in hand, to identify cloud types and the percentage of sky covered by clouds. This information is added to the fact sheet. Every Friday, another team of students transfers the weather data to a computer spreadsheet.

The National Weather Service in Anchorage has access to the weather station via its own modem. Therefore, to make the weather information available to the community and the world, we designed and published our own weather Web page. Current Nikiski weather conditions are posted each afternoon on our weather page. The Web page has attracted interested observers from around the United States. The students are excited to communicate with schools as far away as Florida.

After collecting November weather, we began our first graphing activity, using those temperatures to create a line graph. This was an incredible experience. Even though the students were introduced to graphing in the early grades, they found it very difficult to graph real data. Since that initial experience, the students have selected and graphed weather data on a monthly basis. It has been exciting to watch their ability to analyze data and formulate questions based on their graphs develop and grow over the months.

As a result of this weather project, students are learning to collect, record, analyze, and graph accurate data. They have worked with this project all year, and the level of excitement is as high now as it was in September—or even higher. The students know that their information is valuable and is used by real scientists.

An exciting spin-off activity came about with the use of the global positioning systems. Our elementary school is fortunate in that it is located along a mostly undeveloped lake. This winter, after the lake froze over, I took the students out on the lake every Friday afternoon. We drilled holes through the ice, measured the depth, measured the pH and oxygen levels of the water, and recorded the location according to the global positioning system (GPS).

I then met several students on a Saturday (they just happened to own snow machines) with the purpose of mapping the perimeter of the lake by using the GPS. This led to another interesting mathematics project as several teams of students took GPS readings and created a map of the lake. We now have an accurate drawing of the lake on a grid. The students are working at filling in depth information as it is collected.

According to the manufacturer of the GPS, each second on the GPS represents 33 yards. Another activity we will be working on shortly involves determining the approximate length of the perimeter of the lake. Use of a global positioning system is considered an important life skill in Alaska. As these systems become more and more common in cars, all students could benefit from an understanding of their operation.

In conclusion, creating lessons that are interesting is a key factor toward a successful classroom. When students are totally involved in projects because of their relevance and applicability to their personal lives, learning is enhanced.

Science and Mathematics School Reform

Shirley J. Wright
Pocatello, Idaho

I am deeply concerned about the pressing need and impetus for school reform, especially in the areas of science and mathematics. As a result of the recent TIMSS (Third International Math and Science Study), we at Gate City Elementary School have become aware of a deplorable and alarming lack of excellence in these areas. The study showcases our deficiencies but does little to indicate how to correct them. Teachers are as proficient as their students at creating multiple excuses and explanations for these results. In the end and for whatever reasons, our students are below the international average in most areas of mathematics and science.

The trend toward a more integrated curriculum seems to be a step in the right direction. Not only does integration emphasize that real-world learning does not usually occur as isolated bits of information, but it also encourages the use of higher level thinking skills in applying information in multiple areas to different aspects of a specific topic. Problem-solving skills are nothing more than a game unless they can be applied in a real (or at least realistic) situation.

A significant problem in reform is the lack of time available to teachers for research, reflection, and planning as a team, a building, a district, or a state. Change requires commitment, but commitment requires a basic understanding of the need for change and a knowledge of ways to pursue it. Most of us are sincerely committed to the education of children in the best possible way. Time constraints, however, make it quite difficult for most educators to devote the time necessary to learn how to effect long-term positive change.

Educators function in relative isolation. Greater opportunities for collegiality, both structured and unstructured, would provide a means for some improvement of pedagogy merely through the process of sharing ideas that work. Many teachers tend to be task-oriented rather than goal-oriented. An opportunity to refocus periodically on curriculum goals is beneficial to any program.

We have reached a crucial time when it is essential for all teachers to be cognizant of the need for education reform. We can no longer afford to teach 1 year 25 times. Consensus about precisely what is needed will be difficult to achieve. A willingness to experiment with curricula and methodology, however, will certainly help. National standards, now available in several content areas, are an encouraging sign that change is imminent. We as educators should consider this an exciting opportunity to affect the future.

Helpful Tips

I consider studies of science and the environment to be outstanding fields for interdisciplinary study. If science is considered the study of hows and whys, rather than only the memorization of a specific body of facts, it is inherent in everything we do. The same problem-solving skills used in a study of *Drosophila* genetics can be used in developing a new recipe or repairing an engine. The process of reading develops better reading skills. Children are fascinated with well-chosen nonfiction books. These can be used just as well as fiction to develop critical reading and thinking skills. Be open-minded, tolerant, and creative so that you can be an active participant in the school reform issues ahead of us all.

Importance of Culturally Relevant Curriculums

Elvira Bitsoi Largie
Newcomb, New Mexico

Innovative Method of Teaching Mathematics, Science, and Technology

The method I use in teaching mathematics, science, and technology can be described as teaching concepts in a bilingual maintenance and immersion program. This involves integration of the content areas into one curriculum using a well-balanced approach among the whole language approach, basic skills development, and real-life applications of mathematics, science, and technology. The lessons I teach are relevant and meaningful to the cultures and life of the student population.

An example of the effort to get students interested and remain interested in school is to study the home lives of the students and base lessons that reflect their cultures. These lessons include creating a print-rich environment to produce literate students in two languages, with activities such as field trips, in-school presentations, and parent involvement events. To increase academic skills and abilities, music and computer education are a top priority in my class.

This method and strategy can be summarized and justified as the need to equip bilingual students with a positive self-image, effective abilities, and skills that will allow them to work and survive competently and productively. These students with positive self-esteem who can identify with their cultures will avoid falling into the gap of various cultures and thus keep from turning to alcohol and drugs. Before students fall into the gap, culturally relevant curricula should be implemented in schools.

Educational leaders, curriculum writers, parents, community politicians, and teachers need to realize that knowing one's culture is contentment. This eventually leads to success in learning. I believe that, as an educator, I can influence parents to accept and generate a positive attitude toward the culture of academia if I will allow them to influence me with the wealth of their cultures.

I include cooperative learning and large-group learning involving ongoing research and experiments. Method and curriculum implementation is through thematic units that tie in with the cultures and languages of the students I teach.

Thematic units I have implemented include Navajo Oral Tradition and History—the Water Monster story (the instructional mode and delivery of educational lessons include and reflect on Navajo cultural and traditional teachings regarding the respect for the environment and habitat); Oceanography, Oceans, and Pollution; Sea Life; Endangered Animals and Sea Life; Native American Legends and Beliefs; Science Projects; Rain Forests and Weather; Technology; Field Trips; The Arctic Region; Navajo Farming; Tradition, Culture, and Technology—Corn and the Environment; and Science and Mathematics in Navajo Weaving.

The wonders of the world are brought to the school through classroom lessons that enhance students' awareness about science, mathematics, and technology. A variety of imaginative and interactive activities are a part of the curriculum throughout the year. Students learn about the facts and fascination of animal, plant, and human life by integrating the thematic units with the state benchmarks and the district curriculum.

Parents and the community are involved in lessons that include arts and crafts, lectures, storytelling, hands-on student learning, afterschool enrichment programs, extracurricular activities, and fund-raising events. Theme festivities such as plays/dramas, science projects, and participation on trips culminate all the activities implemented throughout the year.

The strategy in teaching to all learning modes based on the multiple intelligence (MI) theory by Howard Gardner includes cooperative learning, lecture, language arts activities, hands-on experiences, and a variety of whole language and basic skill learning/teaching techniques and methods. This strategy increases the students' language arts skills through relevant and meaningful experiences and develops in them an interest in learning about the world around them with a concentration in mathematics, science, and technology. A language-rich environment with purposeful and supportive communication and the use of print resources and children's literature is an excellent strategy for teaching.

The school district's goals are to increase vocabulary, reading level, and verbal and written expression and to increase the use of technology. Methods in my classroom address the needs of the student population and the goals of the district.

Teaching Methods

My method of teaching is innovative and differs from the traditional method because I think it is my responsibility as a bilingual teacher to ascertain that the school is a place to nurture students so that they will become healthy and contributing adults in a diverse society.

The student population I serve is limited-language proficient and scores below the national norm on standardized test scores. The innovative approach in responding to the specific educational needs of my students is through the implementation of Federal Title 9 Indian Education Program funds for the past 6 years. These funds have made it possible to include educational plans that bring the home lives of students to the school and, in turn, influence the students and parents to study science, mathematics, and technology at home.

One specific project titled "My Sheep at Home and School" included lessons and activities that touched base with the Navajo culture. The students were provided with the opportunity to raise two lambs; through this experience, the students learned that science, mathematics, and technology are a part of their everyday lives (and at the same time met state curriculum requirements).

I believe that, in my classroom, every moment of learning and teaching is like planting in the minds of students' intellectual thoughts, words to live by, and *K'e* (family-kinship) words that will never be lost or forgotten. The students will cherish these teachings. They will never lose their identity or forget their relatives. They will respect where they come from and where they are going in the world of many challenges. They will always have their relatives—*bike daahaloodoo* (Navajo word). They will attain the skills, abilities, and academic minds that will make them confident to learn at higher order thinking levels. They will be strong-minded, healthy, and competent individuals ready to face the challenges in the world of education and society.

Tradition, Culture, and Technology: Corn and the Environment

In this unit, the students learn about history, a positive identity, and relevancy in learning. Learning about corn was planned with the students' history, lifestyle, and present-day livelihood in mind. They learn about their community and local economy. They learn how ethanol is made and how corn and ethanol are sold to other countries.

Technology is integrated beginning with using the word processor, paint and draw programs, spreadsheets, graphing, pictures, and every other possible means to integrate technology. Some students did a popcorn investigation using technology. This investigation determined the brand of popcorn that would pop the most kernels. This popcorn investigation was one that represented our school at the district science and engineering contest. Other programs and software are used as a source for knowledge, comprehension, and evaluation.

The MCI Internet connection that the Milken Foundation provided is very helpful and a rare resource in my community and school. Through this connection, students will experience and learn about the Internet and global information that takes them beyond what the regular classroom and textbooks may have to offer.

CHAPTER **5**

Threading Technology Through the Curriculum

*T*echnology is woven, threaded, and integrated throughout curriculum. Explore how others are doing this.

Chapter Overview

- **Doug Crosby**, a first-grade teacher at Cherry Valley School in Polson, Montana, describes his projects that can be viewed at his school Web site. He shares helpful tips about publishing work on the World Wide Web.

- **Lesa H. Roberts**, a fifth-grade teacher at Farley Elementary in Huntsville, Alabama, offers classroom ideas with scanners, digital cameras, and videodiscs.

- **Loisann B. Huntley**, an assistant principal and fifth-grade teacher at Uncas Elementary School in Norwich, Connecticut, describes an integrated reading, writing, and social studies curriculum for fifth graders. This includes students creating personal timelines of people, events, and geography in their lives.

- **Lonna Sanderson**, a fourth-grade teacher at Graham Elementary School in Austin, Texas, wrote a unit titled "Reptiles: Friends or Foes?" She explains how she effectively uses four classroom computers in teaching about reptiles.

- **Sharon Papineau**, a basic skills teacher/Title I coordinator for Grades 1 to 6 at Washington Elementary School in Valley City, North Dakota, uses technology to develop portfolios. She discusses how she does this by using Kid Pix software.

- **Stacy Kasse**, a fifth-grade teacher at Taunton Forge School in Medford, New Jersey, uses technology to establish a rapport with her students' parents before school begins in the fall.

- **Tammy Payton**, a first-grade teacher and Web editor at Loogootee Elementary West in Loogootee, Indiana, shares technology projects such as "100 E-Mail Messages Around the World."

- **Lynn R. Hobson**, a resource teacher at Maybeury Elementary School in Richmond, Virginia, explains ways technology can be used in teaching. In her school system, technology is an integral component of all areas of the curriculum.

- **Catherine B. Harper**, a second-grade teacher at Tangier Smith Elementary School in Mastic Beach, New Jersey, launched "Tangier TV," a bimonthly show named after Tangier Smith Elementary School. The show seeks to integrate learning in all curricular areas, with features highlighting academic, aesthetic, and social disciplines or issues and focusing them through technology.

- **Kim Mason**, a physical education instructor at Frank Tillery School in Rogers, Arkansas, wanted to stress the importance of daily wellness when seeing the children only twice a week for 25 minutes. "Tillery Kids on Track," a live daily television show aired via closed-circuit cable through the school, was born.

- **Joan L. Anthony**, a third-grade teacher at Hillrise Elementary School in Elkhorn, Nebraska, uses technology with her students to answer the following question: In autumn, do leaves turn color everywhere?

➡ **Sharon C. Locey**, a sixth-grade teacher at Riverside Elementary School in Milwaukie, Oregon, thinks of video production, more often than not, when she thinks of technology.

➡ **Janice S. Catledge**, a teacher of third- and fourth-grade gifted students at Alice Harte Elementary School in New Orleans, Louisiana, uses the Inter"net" to catch butterflies.

▨ First Graders Publishing on the World Wide Web
Doug Crosby
Polson, Montana

I remember the excitement I felt when I first experienced the World Wide Web (WWW) for myself about 3 years ago and immediately identified a whole new audience for my first-grade children.

In my classroom, an intense focus is on early literacy with an underlying philosophy that children learn to read by reading and learn to write by writing. One thing I know about my children is that, to write, they have to have a purpose and an identified audience. The notion of publishing on the Internet for all the world to see was tremendously appealing.

The first project I tackled was a report on a spring field trip to a local university biological field station on Flathead Lake, in the northwest corner of our state. With a digital camera in hand, we all headed out for a fun-filled day of nature hikes and digging in streams to discover the myriad creatures living there; all the while, we snapped pictures. On returning to school, we transferred the pictures into our Web site, and together we wrote captions to accompany the pictures.

Our most touching project was last year when my students developed an ongoing relationship with the residents at a local nursing home. We visited these folks on a regular basis for a few months, each time sharing various literacy activities such as reading books and student-authored stories. Our culminating activity was for the children to interview the residents and ask them about their memories of their own childhoods. Each child created a book based on these experiences. Our last visit of the year was to present these books to our friends at the nursing home and, with the digital camera, to record the event. To document this event on our Web site, we placed the photographs and wrote text to explain what happened.

These and other projects can be viewed at our school Web site at www.digisys.net/cherry, or you can link directly to our classroom page at http://www.digisys.net/cherry/Mr.Crosby_fg.htm. The World Wide Web has given my children another place to share their work and helps reinforce the idea that everything we do should have focus and purpose.

Helpful Tips

To publish work on the WWW, you either need to know all about hypertext markup language (HTML) or use a Web-authoring tool to write it for you. As a busy teacher, I have found the latter technique to be perfect. I use a software from Adobe called PageMill. Other software available include Claris Home Page, and FrontPage by Microsoft. You will also need a server to host your site. Some schools have their own. Ours is hosted by our local Internet provider for free.

A school or district needs to develop a Web publishing policy. We seek parental permission to publish student work on the Internet. We use first names only and do not associate names with photographs. It is important to keep parents informed about Internet projects. I have found Broderbund's Kid Pix an excellent tool to use for publishing student work. After the work is finished, you just select, copy, and paste the work into your Web-authoring software. My future plans for our Web site are to include sound files and QuickTime Virtual Reality software.

Teaching With Technology

Lesa H. Roberts
Huntsville, Alabama

What is technology, and why should it be added to elementary curriculum? Today's curriculum is overflowing. Teachers struggle to meet state and national standards and requirements. Six or seven separate subjects are expected to be introduced to, and mastered by, students every day. How can teaching with technology help either the students or the teacher? The reasons are many and varied. Most important, teaching with technology prepares students for a life in the 21st century. Whether the students work at a fast-food restaurant or fly to a space station, computers will be a part of their lives. Ironically, unlike many adults, children can troubleshoot computer problems even before they learn to write in cursive.

Because PCs are already common in many homes, today's students are literate in computer applications. It takes just a few minutes for most elementary students to learn a new software program. They can use word processors for publishing a wide variety of assignments whenever they choose. Most classrooms have at least one computer, and teachers are comfortable with this technology. The unique technologies are what teachers are finding difficult to integrate into the daily schedule.

One newer technology to find its way into media centers or a few classrooms is the scanner. Scanning allows students to include authentic pictures as part of their research or creative writing. Photographs and illustrations from magazines and resource books can be scanned and saved onto a computer disk to be placed in a text at any time. Even students' artwork can be scanned and placed into creative stories. Photographs as large as 8 × 11 inches can be scanned and reduced to as small as 1 × 1 inch. Photographs can be cropped. For example, if a picture of a herd of elephants is scanned and the student desires just the section that shows one elephant in a watering hole, the photograph can be cut as desired. The computer can also be instructed to focus, straighten, and sharpen the photograph.

Most students easily learn the required process and can find numerous ways to enhance their writing with scanning operations. Scanning a photograph should take a student approximately 5 minutes to complete. The transfer into text is accomplished just as quickly. The rewards are worth the effort! Students get the opportunity to show off their own illustrations, add their school pictures to pen pal letters, and use "real" photographs for research projects, just to name a few options.

Digital cameras eliminate film and negatives, not to mention the price of processing and storage. A digital camera allows you to capture images and then quickly transfer them to a computer so that they can be saved and manipulated by using image-editing software. The camera can be used during field trips, in the classroom, for documenting class presentations, and even to enhance students' writings.

The pictures are stored in the camera until they are downloaded to a computer. Once there, they can be left on the hard drive or on a disk for later use. The pictures can be imported into a writing program or slide show or just printed as pictures with captions. Digital cameras can store anywhere from 16 to more than 100 photographs, depending on the brand and price. It takes about 3 minutes to download the photographs, delete them from the camera, and then begin the process again.

Incorporating videodiscs into the curriculum is one of the easiest but most expensive ways to add technology into the classroom. Videodiscs can be found on a multitude of topics, such as geography and art awareness. All it takes is a laser disc player, a television monitor, and a disc. Unfortunately, this equipment can be very expensive, depending on your choice of hardware and videodiscs. Bar codes are available for many videodisc programs. Bar codes allow students to include visual pictures in their reports and allow teachers to use visuals during presentations. Incorporating bar codes into students' writing is fun and easily accomplished by students as young as 6.

A young author writes a report and tapes the bar codes in the appropriate places on the text. As the report is read, the student scans the bar code and a picture appears on the television screen. Imagine how impressive it is to hear and see such a report. The author is also proud of the work. Writing reports becomes more exciting because the presentation is more fun and extraordinary. Not all videodiscs are interactive, however. Many require the use of a bar code reader and show only one frame at a time until the user chooses to change frames. Other discs play like videos.

More and more students are visual learners today. Incorporation of videodiscs into any curricular area allows visual learners to see and understand what the teacher or another student is trying to explain to them. For example, a teacher can describe how an animal's camouflage helps it survive during different seasons of the year. Telling the students this information is helpful, but showing them pictures on a television monitor allows the students to see the camouflage for themselves and, therefore, remember it.

Classroom Ideas

Scanning

1. *Student Research Projects:* If the students are researching science or social studies topics, allow them time to locate pictures from magazines or texts that can enhance their writing. Library skills can be improved through the students' searches for quality illustrations. The illustrations can be scanned and placed directly into the students' writings.

2. *Classroom Books:* Are the students studying an interesting topic? Allow each student to choose an aspect of the study, scan an illustration, and write a paragraph explaining the importance of the topic. After each student completes the assignment, bind the pages into a book. These books quickly become very popular and are often taken home to show off to parents.

3. *School Photographs:* Scan the students' school-year photos and save them on disks. Use the photographs throughout the year to enhance your classroom newsletters, author pages, and certificates. The students can copy their pictures from the disks onto any writing.

Digital Camera

1. *Document Classroom Activities:* Print each photograph on a separate page and write a caption under each one. Bind the pages together for a class book.

2. *ABC Books:* If your class is studying an interesting topic in science or social studies, allow each student to take one picture, import it into a word processor, and write a caption. Bind the pages for a class book.

3. *Counting Books:* Allow each student to take a picture and write a caption. Bind the pages for a class book.

4. *Create a Slide Show:* Use the photographs to create a slide show. The shows can be shown to the students, to parents during an open house, or on a schoolwide broadcast. Keep your slide shows for the year and have a "year in review" broadcast in May.

5. *Document Field Trips:* Take the digital camera along and take photographs that can be downloaded when you return to school. The students can take the pictures home with them that day to show their parents.

Videodiscs

1. Add bar codes to enhance class presentations.

2. Incorporate videodisc lessons into your instruction for variety.

3. Add bar codes to teacher manuals to reinforce with visuals.

4. Use bar codes and visuals for assessment purposes.

Integrating Reading, Writing, Social Studies, and Technology

Loisann B. Huntley
Norwich, Connecticut

I teach an integrated reading, writing, and social studies curriculum for fifth graders. The overriding idea is that history is the interaction of people, events, and geography. To introduce, build, and intensify this concept, students begin by creating personal timelines of people, events, and geography in their lives up until now, project into the future, and then share with the class.

Next, each student selects one branch of his or her family to study and creates a family tree. This part of the curriculum also teaches students the skill of interviewing, as they must brainstorm and select appropriate questions for the family member who can give them the most information about that branch. Some students can trace their families back to the 1500s, others only to their own grandparents; therefore, how far back one can go is not a criterion for grading the project. The quality of the interview questions and of the interview itself is more important: Higher grades may be given to those students who ask follow-up questions during their interviews. Interviews may be taped, or the students may take notes (not all students have tape recorders available to them). The students are encouraged to share artifacts or family mementos with their classmates.

The first reading component of this curriculum includes a review of the elements of fiction (setting, plot, characters, conflict, climax, resolution) in multicultural folklore. The students select and read as many stories in the genre as possible and report on them. These stories are made available in books, as well as at sites on the Internet. Then, each student selects one folktale from one of his or her countries of origin and, as part of the oral presentation, tells that story. The students may read or act out their memorized stories. Generally, students who memorize and act out their stories receive higher grades. Some years, most students read their stories; other years, most memorize and tell them. Each group of students has its strengths.

The geography component of this curriculum teaches students to use interactive CDs—in particular, Virtual Globe or World Atlas. They are required to trace, on the map provided, the path their ancestors took to come to Norwich and, if appropriate and possible, tell why they came to this country. They are encouraged to search the software for interesting multimedia snippets to share about their countries of origin. As the students practice and finally present, they are learning what is available in the software program, improving their mouse skills, and learning that the computer can be used as a presentation tool as well as a research tool. Clearly, this part of the curriculum encourages students to take pride in their heritage and to respect the heritage of their classmates and nurtures a feeling of belonging at home and in the classroom.

Next, we venture into our study of the 20th century. We are spiraling out gradually from ourselves (personal timelines), to our families (heritage project), and now to our century. The students are given a brief overview of some major events of the 20th century, and then they select partners (or the teacher can pair students) and a topic for in-depth research. Not all major events can be addressed, and the teacher selects those events on the basis of board of education goals or whatever criteria are appropriate.

For the first time, students use a research process—from taking notes on index cards from books and writing a bibliography, to taking notes from selected Internet sites and interactive CDs such as Multimedia American History and encyclopedias such as Encarta. They must identify key words for their topic in order to search effectively. They must begin to learn to read and evaluate more difficult material and decide whether it is important or useful to their topic. Some students may require assistance, and the help of paraprofessionals in an inclusion model is effective in this situation as they assist students in reading and interpreting information.

Finally, the students transform information by writing interviews to tell about the people, events, and geography (returning to that basic idea) related to their topics. This task prevents writing reports, which is often just copying, allows students to practice again the skill of interviewing, and forces them to identify and select important information. An example is that, in the final oral presentation, one student is a reporter and the other a *Titanic* survivor or Wilbur Wright or John F. Kennedy or another appropriate person.

Just before the students do their presentations, each picks a red or black checker from a hat or box. Red is for reporter; black is for interviewee. This chance drawing requires both students in a pair to write the interview and know the information. Then they do their prepared interviews, and they are videotaped for them to watch and evaluate later. Each of the students writes an action plan that includes three things they would continue to do in their next project and three things they would like to improve. At the end of their taped presentations, student pairs tell me what the pivotal date is for their topic. For instance, December 17, 1903, was the first successful flight by Orville and Wilbur Wright. I write these in order on the chalkboard, and the culminating activity is to have students in teams of four create and illustrate a 20th-century timeline including the pivotal dates in chronological order. This project also builds on the presentation skill used for creating their first personal timelines.

At the same time, we are reading two of our required books—*Sadako and the Thousand Paper Cranes,* and *The Lion, the Witch, and the Wardrobe*—both of which take place during World War II. Reading discussions are based on the themes of world peace and good versus evil. An enjoyable method is to conduct a graded oral assessment. Questions are higher level: requiring comparing and contrasting, evaluating reasons for the actions of characters, and requiring students to explain the meanings of events. One writing prompt requires the students to tell why they believe in world peace; in another, they are asked to identify, compare, and contrast the good and evil characters in *The Lion, the Witch, and the Wardrobe,* giving examples of the characters' behavior and speech to back up their answers. Another requires them to answer the question, How did war affect, or change, the lives of Sadako and the four children in *The Lion, the Witch, and the Wardrobe*?

This comprehensive, 10-week curriculum unit combines processes, skills, and content in a meaningful way for students. The computer and other technology are used in several ways, but never exclusively as a research or presentation tool. The students still like to create hands-on products, such as timelines, by using traditional art materials.

Very often, former students have explained the project to their younger siblings before coming to fifth grade. When I tell the younger brothers and sisters they are allowed to study and use information from their older sibling's family tree made in my class, they tell me it is still hanging up in their room! This is the best compliment of all—that this learning had such long-term meaning for students.

It is important to evaluate the students on many different components of this unit, including note taking, oral presentations, computer skills, and hands-on products, and to set up criteria for earning an average or above-average grade: for instance, as mentioned previously, to give an average grade to students who read their folktales and a higher grade to those who memorize it and act it out. When given such choices, the students will often seek the highest grade they can, at least in the areas they perceive as their strengths. This begins to build personal responsibility for choosing excellence.

I believe that I won the Connecticut Teacher of the Year Award because the project (a) is imbued with personal meaning for students, (b) integrates technology as research and presentation tools, rather than treats it as a separate entity, and (c) is a comprehensive and well-thought-out curriculum unit. I hope it will inspire teachers to adopt or adapt a similar unit for teaching their students respect and pride in self, family, and country.

Internet Sites and Resources

Mythology and Folklore:
http://pubweb.acns.nwu.edu/pib/mythfolk.htm

Cranes for Peace: http://www.he.net/sparker/cranes.html

Yahoo: http://www.yahoo.com (Select Social Science:History: US History: 20th century or People; then students must look for individual topics.)

USA Page: http://www.msstate.edu/Archives/History/USA/usa.html (Select: 20th century or People or individual topics, including a separate list for wars.)

Other Resources Required

Interactive CDs, including an encyclopedia, MultiMedia U.S. History, American History (Multi Educator), Software Toolworks World Atlas.

Books: Sadako and the Thousand Paper Cranes by Eleanor Coerr;
The Lion, the Witch, and the Wardrobe by C. S. Lewis

Other books to act as basic resources

Helpful Tips

Time is the rare commodity in getting students on-line with one Internet-accessible computer and a telephone line. However, many students are willing to give up their recess at least once a week and to stay after school when they can to work on technology-related projects. The creation of Web pages has been an exciting, ongoing part of our classroom work. Visit our forever-under-construction site: http://www.connix.com/rclement.

Reduce the number of assignments that are graded. This encourages the students to explore, make mistakes and learn from them, and ultimately become self-directed learners. Instead, have the students look at each assignment as part of a process they are involved in to increase skills. Have them evaluate each body of work they complete: We call them action plans. Quite simply, each student writes three things he or she would continue to do and three things he or she would like to improve when completing the next project.

Do not make all centers or methods of learning involve technology. For instance, we always have a jigsaw puzzle relating to content area curriculum available for students to work on as a goal once each day. The same is true for projects. Many students enjoy working with their hands as much as they enjoy videotaping a presentation or using Hyper-Studio software. Assessment should involve many media and methods for evaluation.

Think of the classroom more as a workplace than as a "traditional" classroom. Work is ongoing, and a balance must be found between giving the students a body of knowledge with closure and giving them continued opportunities to expand knowledge and skills in an "open loop." Both are important, and finding this balance will be challenging in the years to come.

We have an Acceptable Use Policy that students, parents, and teachers sign, and we have never had a problem. The students want to use the Internet and follow rules very carefully, at least in fifth grade. Still, teachers must provide controls and be vigilant and aware of what students are accessing.

Units of Practice Integrating Technology

Lonna Sanderson
Austin, Texas

What is a tuatara? To find out, my students used a Macintosh computer to watch "Tuatara," a ClarisWorks slide show created by three of their classmates. Through text, sound, pictures, and maps, information about the tuatara, a "living fossil" reptile that exists only in New Zealand, was presented.

During the 1997-98 school year, I was one of the Austin Independent School District's 25 MAESTRO (Mentoring Austin Educators for Success with Technology as a Regular Occurrence) teachers and received extensive training in integrating technology into the curriculum. I learned to write units of practice that integrate technology into the core curriculum. One unit that I wrote is "Reptiles: Friends or Foes?"

I had taught a science/language arts unit on reptiles to my fourth-grade students for several years. My way of teaching it was fairly traditional: Every student read an article I wrote about each type of reptile, answered questions and filled in crossword puzzles about the article, viewed and took notes from the same videos and laser discs, and then selected one reptile to research in detail and gave a report to the class. Even though the students always enjoyed this unit, I thought that the way I taught it was a bit tedious and boring.

My first question in rewriting this unit was, "How can I effectively use my four classroom computers in teaching about reptiles?" The answer was, "Divide the class into seven groups and assign each group a type of reptile to research. The reptile types will be sea turtles, land turtles, freshwater turtles, crocodilians, snakes, lizards, and the tuatara. Each group will create a ClarisWorks slide show and make an oral presentation to teach their classmates all about that type of reptile. I will not present any information; I will simply facilitate their work, teach the technology skills they need, and help them find resources."

During a class discussion, the students listed subtopics that were placed on a note-taking chart for each group to use during the research phase of the project. Sources of information included CD-ROM encyclopedias, animal CD-ROM titles, books, magazine articles, videos, and World Wide Web sites about reptiles. (My school had no Internet access, so I used WebWhacker software at home to download sites for the students to view at school.) The students also wrote letters to zoos and organizations, asking for information and pictures. After gathering information, the students created their slide shows.

I introduced the basic steps to creating slide shows to all the students in the computer lab. Then I wrote directions for student groups to follow while using the classroom computers. Each group planned its slides on paper and then created them on a computer. They inserted pictures and QuickTime movies from CD-ROM sources and World Wide Web sites, inserted still pictures and videos from videos I took during a field trip and in the classroom, added voice narration, and composed and formatted text. During a class discussion, the students created a rubric to use for judging the slide shows.

Student groups also planned and made oral presentations to the class. Again, the goal for each group of students was to teach others all about the type of reptile it researched. One group created a puppet show. Some groups showed parts of videos or laser discs. Some showed live reptiles, and some showed pictures. All the groups created visual aids, such as posters or transparencies, to enhance their presentations. The class used another class-developed rubric for judging the presentations. I videotaped each presentation, and students critiqued their presentation techniques while viewing the tape.

While implementing this unit of practice, I realized I would never again teach the unit in the traditional way. My students learned more about reptiles than previous students had, learned to work effectively with others to accomplish goals and meet deadlines, and learned to use technology as a tool for gathering information and making presentations.

I have written additional units of practice about prehistoric native Texans and bats. In both units, students make presentations using HyperStudio software. One feature of the bat unit is that it is cumulative; each year, my students add cards to the existing stack, building on the work of students in previous classes. Perhaps someday I'll have a HyperStudio stack with a card for every type of bat in the world!

Helpful Tips

Even though I had seven groups working with four classroom computers, we had no problems with access to the computers. While some
groups used the computers, others did research in the library or classroom, took notes from videos and laser discs, wrote letters, and/or revised
printed copies of their slides.

I knew little about using the slide show feature of ClarisWorks and
learned along with my students. One group's slide show kept causing
the computer to freeze. I did not know why but noticed that the left
margin marker in the menu bar had been moved far to the right, creating
a very narrow page. After completely redoing their slide show twice, the
frustrated students learned to leave the margin marker at the default
setting.

Because my students enjoyed the project so much, they worked cooperatively and had few disputes. I assigned two or three students to
each group. Larger groups seem to have much more difficulty staying
on task, dividing the work, and making decisions about the appearance
and content of the slides. To ensure that each student became proficient
in using the ClarisWorks slide show features, I required each group
member to create two or more slides.

Equipment and software I used:

> Four Macintosh PowerPC computers with CD-ROM drives (one
>   with video-in capability)
>
> Laser disc player
>
> Video camera
>
> Printer
>
> Zip drive (This was useful when transferring slide shows from one
>   computer to another. Slide shows were too large to fit on a
>   diskette.)
>
> ClarisWorks software

CD-ROM encyclopedias

Animal and science CD-ROM titles

CD-ROM atlases

WebWhacker software

Scan converter (This was used to connect the computer to television for class viewing of slide shows.)

Equipment I did not have that would have been useful:

Digital camera

Color scanner

Developing Portfolios for Title I and the Classroom

Sharon Papineau
Valley City, North Dakota

Accountability and assessment are the important buzzwords for education. I have been looking for ways to help assess my students by using technology. My project is using Kid Pix slide show software to note the progress of Title I students, along with involving the parents.

I set a new goal at the beginning of each school year. These goals include the encouragement of writing, parental tutoring, reading books and magazines for pleasure, and now using technology in my classroom.

This year, I asked one student to develop his own portfolio with his parents' help. A storybook plan was sent home so that the student and his parents could develop a plan for making a Kid Pix slide show. The student submitted a writing titled "Who Am I," which included a paragraph about his family life. He brought pictures of his family and a picture of his favorite activity, which is riding horses. I scanned into the computer the writing materials, samples of his classroom work, and pictures for the slide show. This student designed a "moopie" (part of a Kid Pix slide show) with his own creative drawings and selected a movie about wildlife. He recorded his writing "Who Am I?" and explained the pictures. The moopie has selected music from Kid Pix.

My student did not lose any classroom time, as he came in early to do this project and to review reading vocabulary words for that day. I received special permission from the student and his parents to show his slide presentation. Now we will be able to build on his portfolio each year, and he will submit new writing samples of work to add to his slide show until sixth grade. His parents will be able to observe the progression of his work. My student has excitedly shared this project with his peers, and they, too, are eager to do this project.

I have also developed a slide show for the first, second, and third grades. The students prepared writings, and I took pictures of the students, using the QuickTake camera, that were later transferred into the computer. The students recorded their writings and their names for their pictures. Parents can observe the slide show at the annual Parent Open House.

This year served as a trial period and introduction to a Kid Pix-based portfolio for each student enrolled in the Title I program. Next year, I will start with first- and second-grade students and extend it to third graders if possible. Each student will have his or her own private portfolio using the slide show. I think that Kid Pix is a wonderful tool for the students and families to track the children's progression.

The students use computers extensively when possible. I have enrolled students in a program called "Computer Curriculum Corporation." For example, a student works on mathematics or reading for 10 minutes at his instructional level. The computer gives a history of the work completed, along with the grade level at which the student is functioning. If he is having great difficulty with a specific skill, the computer can print out worksheets focusing in that area so that the student can practice until he masters that skill.

Inspiration, another computer program, is used to develop critical-thinking skills and enhance comprehension. Graphical organizing, concept mapping, and webbing of main ideas and characters inspire the students to develop ideas and to organize thinking.

Living Books software has whet the appetite for pleasure reading. The students excitedly come in early to work with this program. The students use Kid Works 2 to practice spelling and to write stories. They can add imaginative drawings to their stories.

The students anxiously work on a wide variety of projects using technology. This has added greatly to their joys of learning.

Parents and Teachers: A New Conferencing Method?

Stacy Kasse
Medford, New Jersey

Each school year ends with Pass Up Day. This is a time when teachers can see who is assigned to their homerooms, and students can meet their teachers. It alleviates a lot of the summer "I don't know who my teacher is" anxiety for students and allows me to plan for the upcoming crop of fifth-grade students.

This last Pass Up Day, I devised a clozed letter for my students to fill out. This gave me some insight into the group. That night, after I returned home, I typed a form letter, inserted some of the information I had received, and sent it immediately to my students' parents, telling them how excited I was to have their children in my class. Many students had given me their e-mail addresses (a first), and with that information I contacted their homes.

Parents were delighted to hear from me via e-mail. They expressed their thanks and proceeded to answer the question I had asked them: "What can we do to make this the best year your child has ever had in school?" I don't know when I have ever had such insightful answers. The parents were up-front with their suggestions, and throughout the summer we e-mailed back and forth without their children knowing what we were doing. The parents were very happy to know that they could contact me throughout the year to keep in touch by using this method.

How wonderful it is to be going into the classroom this year having already established a rapport with my parents and knowing their expectations. I couldn't have achieved this over the telephone. The use of technology set me up for a great year.

CLOZED LETTER THAT STUDENTS FILLED OUT FOR PASS UP DAY

June 1997

Dear Ms. Kasse,

My name is _____, and I had _____ as a
teacher in fourth grade. I am _____ about being in your class next
year. I would like to tell you a few things about myself.

The first thing you should know is that I love _____.
This is my very favorite thing to do in life. In fact, if I didn't have to go to
school, I would be doing this every day.

At home, I live with my _____ and my brothers and
sisters, _____. I have _____ pets.
They are _____.

The next thing you should know is that I really dislike _____.
It would be my wish that this could be eliminated from my life once and for all.

The last book I read was _____.
I found that this book was _____ for me to read. I really _____
reading and wish I could do _____ of it.

If I could change one thing about my reputation in school, it would be that
people would think I was _____. I feel this way because

_____ .

I really _____ writing. It's _____ for me to write.
I know you do much writing in fifth grade, so I know I'll adapt.

In fifth grade, I really need to work on my _____ .
I know I could be better at it if _____.

I _____ have a computer at home. My e-mail address is
_____ (only if you know it and have one).

I would _____ like to become a pen pal to a student in Australia this summer. I know that you are going to Australia to teach. My address, should someone want to write to me, is

_____

_____

_____

(Please fill this in even if you don't want a pen pal.)

In conclusion, I _____ looking forward to this vacation. I plan on _____

_____

_____

I will see you in September with my notebook filled with paper, pens, pencils, clipboard, and other things I know will make my life easier. Have a great summer, and see you then.

Sincerely,

_____

Age: _____ Birthdate: _____

Parents' names: _____

Telephone number: _____

Sample of Letter Sent Home to Parents Following Pass Up Day

Ms. S. Kasse
Home Telephone
E-mail: skasse@aol.com

August 23, 1997

Mr. and Mrs. _____
Medford, NJ 08055

Dear Mr. and Mrs. _____ :
    You have a bright 10-year-old! I say that with assurance because
I'm going to be Michael's teacher next year. I enjoyed having Michael in
my class for Pass Up Day.
    Using Michael's love of sports, we can get him to read some great
books this summer. Because he plans to go to Canada, the Virgin Islands,
and Pittsburgh, perhaps he could write some great stories to help him
get some practice with writing.
    Michael has expressed an interest in becoming a pen pal to one of
my students in Australia this summer. With your approval, I will give out
his address.
    I am writing to tell you that I welcome comments and suggestions
from the parents of my students. Please don't hesitate to contact me if
you'd like to discuss something. A telephone call or an e-mail is always
appreciated.
    It is with pleasure that I get to know your family. I hope that you
have a wonderful and safe summer.

    Sincerely,
    Stacy Kasse

▨ Technology Projects

Tammy Payton
Loogootee, Indiana

In the spring of 1996, my school administrators asked me whether I was interested in creating our school Web page. Well, that Web page has turned into a Web site: http://www.siec.k12.in.us/west. It is amazing how our school Web site has taken on a life of its own! Our site has won recognition on the Internet, and I was involved in interviews with educational Web sites as well as local, regional, and national newspapers. Also, I have received invitations to train other area educators on Internet applications.

After I introduce the Internet to my children, I have them search for information beginning with every letter of the alphabet. You can go to this Web page and see this lesson: http://www.siec.k12.in.us/west/proj/abcless.htm.

When my children understand how to search for information, I have them publish projects on the Internet. One project my children have done is to create a quiz about President Abraham Lincoln. You can see this published project at http://www.siec.k12.in.us/west/proj/lincoln. The lesson won Microsoft Encarta's grand prize in the Teacher Lesson Collection Contest.

The children are learning that they can research for information, publish information, and collaborate. One of the most enjoyable projects we have done is "Monster Project." By working with a school in London, England, the children wrote and drew descriptions of four monsters while London's schoolchildren did the same. We have exchanged these descriptions and are comparing and contrasting how well we described our monsters so that the London children could draw them by only using our descriptions. You can see this project at http://www.siec.k12.in.us/west/proj/monster.

Currently, I am hosting my first collaborative project called "100 E-Mail Messages Around the World." More than 400 schools from around the world are participating. Literally thousands of students are participating in this project, which visually demonstrates how the Internet brings the world to our doorstep. By combining global communication skills with geography and social studies, this simple project can demonstrate the global outreach the Internet offers to all schools. You can see this project at http://www.siec.k12.in.us/west/proj/100th.

Helpful Tips

The biggest challenge we as teachers have in education is to take abstract concepts and tie concrete examples to them. With the Internet project "100 E-Mail Messages Around the World," students, staff, and parents can see how the Internet brings the world to our door by mapping on large wall maps the greetings sent to them.

Challenging students to take an active role with their learning guarantees success. Whether it's reenacting the Revolutionary War or creating a stage where the county courtroom is played, students who are actively participating learn more than those who passively learn facts from textbooks.

Enhance and Extend Learning Using Technology

Lynn R. Hobson
Richmond, Virginia

In my school system, technology is an integral component of instruction in all areas of the curriculum. From calculators to computers to laser disc players, students from kindergarten through fifth grade use technology to enhance and extend their learning. Although I am currently an elementary resource teacher, during my last 2 years in the classroom I specialized in teaching mathematics and science to fifth graders in both gifted and heterogeneously mixed groups. Whenever possible, I tried to integrate mathematics, science, and technology to provide engaging, meaningful learning experiences for my students.

For one successful lesson, I used learning stations during a science unit on plant processes. The class was divided into cooperative groups, with one student from each group responsible for researching one of the plant processes being studied: photosynthesis, transpiration, respiration, and reproduction. While one group used the World Book Multimedia Encyclopedia, various science CD-ROMs, or reference books for research, other groups began work on a HyperStudio stack including pictures and information from their research. They also made posters illustrating the plant processes and entered information about specific plants into a Plant Taxonomy database. The students conducted plant growth experiments and recorded data on spreadsheets, which allowed them to create graphs to display the results of their experiments.

When studying animals, my students used the database application in Microsoft Works 4.0 to compile information gleaned from their research on a specific animal. Fields were created for recording the animal's name, whether it was a vertebrate or invertebrate, its class, kingdom, scientific name, habitat, and prey. The students could then sort and filter the information to find common traits among the animals.

HyperStudio is one of the favorite programs at our school and can be used in conjunction with almost any science unit. For example, the students could draw the human digestive system and label the major organs. The animation feature could be used to show the path of a piece of food as it moves through the system. During a unit on matter, one group imported a picture of the periodic table, making each square into an active button. By clicking on the name of an element, the students could move to a card that included specific information and an atomic model of the element. One student even used animation to show the electrons rotating around the nucleus.

My students also participated each spring in a National Geographic Kidsnet unit on solar energy. They used a computer to telecommunicate with students all over the world about how solar energy is used in their communities, and in the process they learned and used geography, science, language arts, and technology skills.

Calculators and computers were an important part of my mathematics program as well. Basic four-function and fraction calculators were readily available for students to use to perform tedious calculations, for problem solving, and in concept development. Contrary to the fears of many, using calculators does not prevent students from acquiring basic mathematics skills; in fact, it often enhances mathematics instruction by allowing them to explore worthwhile problems beyond their computational skills. Using the MECC MathKeys software series, students had frequent opportunities to use computers to explore the concepts of whole numbers, fractions and decimals, geometry, and probability and to build connections between the concrete and the symbolic levels of mathematics.

In addition to the advantages of using technology with students, there are benefits for teachers as well. I created an electronic gradebook by using the spreadsheet application of Microsoft Works 4.0 software, which saved me many hours of manually computing the students' grades at the end of each marking period. Once the students' names and the subjects I taught were set up on the spreadsheet, I entered formulas that automatically calculated each student's average whenever a new grade was added. The database application in Microsoft Works was used to keep track of student information and could even be merged with word processing documents to individualize form letters to parents.

I have only scratched the surface of all the exciting ways technology can be used in teaching. If you are just beginning to explore this area, I advise you to start slowly. I guarantee, though, that once you get the "bug," you'll find countless ways to integrate technology with your curriculum.

Videolearning

Catherine B. Harper
Mastic Beach, New Jersey

It occurred to me one summer day 3 years ago that, more than any other generation, the students I taught were "children of the screen": video games, computers, VCRs, and televisions. The thought following this vacation-induced revelation was the challenge: Why not frame instruction in a form that these techno-savvy young scholars would find a natural mode? In fact, why not involve them in every aspect of presenting learning on a screen?

With my principal's blessing, two small grants for sundry materials, a donated camcorder with an LCD screen, and a souped-up VCR (with flying eraseheads for assemble editing) donated by the PTO, I launched Tangier TV (TTV), named after Tangier Smith Elementary School, a K-5 public school. TTV is the ultimate lesson plan, the convergence of teaching and technology in a student-empowered way, joining learners with learners, as well as learners with their families and the community. It is technology, not for technology's sake, but rather as it enhances and extends learning.

Each bimonthly show is about 30 minutes long, taped on 8-mm film and edited onto standard VHS tape. The production is in a magazine format, meaning that two students introduce a series of related packages, or short taped segments. My spirited crew consists of an assignment editor (who shares the responsibilities in producing each show), reporters, field correspondent (an off-campus reporter), science editor, production assistants (who facilitate setting up equipment and taping), and anchors. We meet regularly to plan each show, balancing the program to include participation of as many grade levels as possible. They pitch their ideas or ones that peers or teachers have suggested, propose ways to present the packages, and volunteer for assignments. Truly, this is an educational mission for kids, by kids, and of kids.

TTV seeks to integrate learning in all curricular areas, with features highlighting academic, aesthetic, and social disciplines or issues, focusing them through technology. For example, one package was "The Great Fifth-Grade Gum Survey." This presentation involved students from a special education class applying surveying techniques, analyzing and reporting the results in graph form (mathematics), working cooperatively to prepare and present copy (social skills, language arts), and understanding the parameters of video recording in preparing their presentation (technology). One popular feature is "Ask Mother Nature": Students curious about any natural phenomena can pose their questions to the TTV science editor (a.k.a. Mother Nature), who engages peers, teachers, literature, and other appropriate resources in researching her answers. She reports each question and answer in a package complete with a demonstration of the scientific principles involved.

As executive producer, I provide the organizational structure, know-how, and networking necessary for each show, guiding the students to the sources they need, assisting them with their scripts in an editorial capacity. I'm also the videographer, as TTV is a no-budget enterprise that cannot afford the camcorder meeting an accidental demise by a distracted fourth-grade production assistant. To meet the demands of these roles, I interned for an intense day at a local commercial television station, read video-related books, subscribed to *Videomaker* magazine, attended a national video convention, and taught myself how to videotape. Of course, the most valuable action I took was to draft my husband, Robert, as technical assistant for editing together all the video footage. Even with his technical expertise, it takes the greater part of a Saturday to edit a half-hour show.

TTV is a labor-intensive enterprise on my part. Student meetings and tapings are done before school, during my lunchtime or prep period, or after school. I may spend hours working with a student or small groups as they shape and rehearse a package. Their growing command of the learning they present and its successful reception by the school's 1,300 viewers is most gratifying.

Two major frustrations in terms of the resulting quality are using consumer rather than profe$$ional equipment and working within the constraints of no budget. The students have Spielbergesque visions, and I have to figure out how to create videomagic with a $499 camcorder whose internal microphone was never designed to catch the soft tones of a shy kindergartner.

Each show has managed to transcend such dilemmas, however, and to showcase entire classes and individual students introducing learning in an exciting and motivating way. Sometimes their message is powerful and profound. In TTV's first season, a fifth grader wrote to me, "I think I should be on TTV so I can tell all the kids how good reading is and how it changed my life." On screen, this student was most convincing in a way I don't think I ever could be.

Tillery Kids on Track

Kim Mason
Rogers, Arkansas

"T.K.O.T." is a live daily television show aired via closed-circuit cable through the school where I teach. The idea originated one year during National Physical Fitness and Sport Month. I wanted to know how I could stress (model) the importance of daily wellness when seeing the students only twice a week for 25 minutes. With the support of the administration, we hooked a video camera into a cable box and connected to a few televisions in strategic places throughout the building to allow viewing by more than 600 students. This process allowed all students to be actively involved at the same time each day.

The success of this project led to the PTA funding more equipment—a television in each classroom. Parental help resulted in cable being dropped into each room, and our studio venture began. Within 4 years, our equipment inventory, with help from local organizations and some technology funding, grew to (in addition to the classroom televisions) three video cameras, a video mixer, a title maker, four monitors, a computer with a scan converter, and three VCRs!

The studio is operated totally by students. Each year, interested students fill out job applications. Each includes vital information, references, letters of recommendation, and a short essay. Applicants are then screened, interviewed, and given an opportunity to perform a "screen" or "tech" test. A crew of 12 is chosen. Responsibilities range from technical to on-camera roles. The students go through training before the season begins. This becomes the "core" crew, but hundreds of children are seen on "T.K.O.T." One goal is to allow as many as possible to be "featured" on the show. This year's crew consists of two fifth graders, eight fourth graders, and two third graders. We go for responsible, creative, and willing students; grade/age is not a criterion.

The format of the show includes basic "housekeeping things"—for example, announcements, weather, menu, and sports/warm-up activity. Then, each day, we add a few features. These include segments on the environment, character development, special readers, sign language, Spanish, new students, teachers' brag time, favorite things (movies, books, games), Name That Tune, trivia time, and mind puzzles. The capability of hooking the computer to the mixer and pulling up Web pages to transmit to the classrooms has added a new feature to the show. The Tillery Toad (a puppet) is the "flow-master" that helps with transition throughout the show. In addition to the daily show, we air some live special events—for example, class projects and the school spelling bee. Our "roving" reporters and camera crew also get events on video and air clips during the show.

My initial motive was to reach as many students as possible and to share fitness and sports with them. The opportunity has surpassed my intentions! It is a true "wellness" show. Not only does it create camaraderie throughout the building, but it also hits the areas of wellness that I stress with my classes. Being fit is more than being physical.

Helpful Tips

- Guide the students to channel their energy. It is OK for the students to be active.

- Be real. Walk the talk.

- Be consistent.

- Realize that education is a lifelong process.

- Allow students to think for themselves, but give them the appropriate framework to do so.

- Know that it takes everyone—home, school, and church—working together.

- Do not get so caught up in the mental and physical that the emotional and spiritual suffer.

- Promote quality daily physical education. It can change a school while giving life skills to the students.

- Move to learn and learn to move!

Finding Fall

Joan L. Anthony
Elkhorn, Nebraska

As the September weather in Nebraska turned cooler and fall sports and falling leaves were in the air, my third-grade students began to wonder whether leaves were turning color everywhere. Although they "knew" that climates were different, they had no experiences to challenge their assumption that "fall" was the same everywhere—changing weather and leaf color. "Finding Fall" began as a telecommunications project in which we could collect and analyze data about fall weather and the accompanying seasonal changes.

Through a message on a listserv for educators, other classes were invited to join us for a 6-week project. Once a week, classes would send us their noon temperatures, sunrise/sunset times, observations of a tree on their school grounds, and any other seasonal observations they wanted to share. I compiled all the weekly data and sent them to each participating school.

Each week, the students eagerly waited for the data to be distributed. Small pictures of leaves of our partner schools' trees, drawn by my children from their partners' descriptions, were placed on a large wall map. As new data came in, old data were taken down and glued, chronologically, on large sheets of construction paper.

Over the week, patterns began to develop, and my children's ideas began to change. Schools from Texas, California, Hawaii, and Florida told us of warm temperatures, green trees, mangoes and coconuts, and new flowers. Schools from Canada and Alaska told us of much colder temperatures and trees with no leaves. My children discovered a connection between leaf color and falling temperatures. Through an Internet experience, the children constructed their own learning about weather and seasons.

Content Standard A of the "National Science Education Standards" states, "As a result of activities in grades K-4, all students should develop:

> *abilities necessary to do scientific inquiry*
> *understanding about scientific inquiry"*
> (pp. 121-123)

Standard 11: Statistics and Probability of the "Curriculum and Evaluation Standards for School Mathematics" also shares the importance of authentic data collection activities in the K-4 curriculum. Using computer technology, children and teachers can become actively involved in authentic, interdisciplinary data collection projects from which information can be collected, analyzed, and shared.

Using computer technology to assist in data collection projects necessitates flexibility! Computer are not things to be used just to fill time when children have completed assignments, nor should computers be used solely for high-tech "drill and kill" practice. Teachers must look objectively at their units and decide what can be done more meaningfully, effectively, and efficiently with computer technology.

Searching for and discovering weather patterns by using the World Wide Web is more effective than reading about such patterns in a textbook. Students can learn about similarities and differences between students, schools, and communities through e-mail. Virtual reality movies can be used to share field trips or constructions of simple machines. Learning can be shared on a classroom's Web page. Students can research animals, hear their sounds, and watch a related movie on the Web and include this learning in a multimedia presentation. The latest information about space exploration is available on the World Wide Web.

Does all of this sound too complicated, too time-consuming, or as if it requires too much teacher knowledge? Just start small. Choose one topic that sounds manageable—maybe communicating occasionally with key pals or using e-mail to find out about the modes of transportation used by students to get to school. Join listservs for educators where teachers share ideas and ask for participants in teacher-student-initiated projects. Then learn along with your students and enjoy their excitement! The excitement is contagious! Web site is http://205.202.101.100/Hillrise/hillrise.html.

⬛ Teaching With Video Technology

Sharon C. Locey
Milwaukie, Oregon

Many people think of computers when they see the word *technology*. But, when I think of technology, more often than not video production comes to mind. I have found that one of the quickest ways to motivate students is to put a video camera in their hands and turn our classroom into a production studio.

My students and I produce a biweekly television news magazine show called "The Riverside Report." We feature events happening in the school, spotlight individual classrooms and students, and present our version of "man-on-the-street" sound bites. We also send student reporters into the community to do field reports about local businesses. For example, when our students were learning about bowling in physical education class, we sent a reporter to a local bowling center to get a look at what goes on behind the pins. We also include commercials in our show, but unlike traditional advertising, our students create 30-second spots about character traits such as honesty, integrity, respect, patriotism, and courage. "The Riverside Report" is aired on our local cable access station several times daily so that people in our community can learn more about what's happening in our school and see what great things our students are doing and thinking about today.

We use the video camera for many other exciting classroom projects as well. Instead of traditional social studies reports, my students present newscasts about the countries they have researched. Or they create mock travel agencies and produce videos about the countries they are trying to persuade their client (me!) to travel to.

Traditional book reports can get boring for students by the time they are in sixth grade. So my students record book commercials or do "Siskel & Ebert"-type book reviews on video.

Many teachers have their students play mock versions of "Jeopardy" or other game shows as culminating activities, but my class goes a step further. We convert the classroom into a game show set, videotape the whole event (complete with studio audience!), and air it on cable access.

I also use video to enhance the students' writing and literary skills. My students write a movie every year. They know all about plot, character, setting, foreshadowing, climax, and resolution because their movie would not make any sense without those elements.

When you think about technology, do not limit yourself to computers. Think video technology too, and your students will be glad you did.

Helpful Tips

- Prevent cutting off your subject's first and last words by making sure you begin recording 5 seconds before he or she speaks, and continue recording 5 seconds after he or she finishes speaking.

- If your subject stands in front of a window or bright light, it will be too dark to see. If you can't shoot elsewhere, press the "back light" button continuously on your camcorder; it won't solve the problem, but it will help.

- If you do not have microphones other than the one on the camcorder, stand close enough to your subject for the camcorder to pick up the words, and ask your subject to speak up! Also be aware of nearby background noise the camera may catch that you don't want on your video.

- Use the "fade" button at the beginning and end of your scenes to make your transitions smoother.

- Use music whenever you can. Many camcorders have an audio dub feature that lets you add music to your video after you finish shooting.

- If you have trouble holding the camcorder still, use a tripod to steady the camcorder, making your video look much more professional.

- Do not make your viewers seasick. Only use the "zoom-in/zoom-out" buttons when truly necessary and appropriate while you're recording.

- Have fun! Stay relaxed, don't panic, and remember that you can usually reshoot a scene if you have to.

Using the Inter "Net" to Catch Butterflies

Janice S. Catledge
New Orleans, Louisiana

Our school is on the migration route for monarch butterflies as they fly south to Mexico in the fall and north in the spring. Some butterflies travel 2,500 miles from their summer breeding grounds to over-wintering sites in the mountains of Mexico. Scientists still have many questions about how monarchs accomplish this amazing migration.

With funding from a grant, my class planted a butterfly garden, including milkweed as host plants for the monarchs, as well as nectar plants. Monarchs will lay eggs only on milkweed because it is the only plant their caterpillars will eat. The first year, my students were thrilled to observe their very hungry caterpillars transforming themselves into jeweled chrysalides and then into beautiful butterflies.

The students asked many questions for which I had no answers. I was excited to read that an Internet site (http://www.ties.k12.us/jnorth) was electronically tracking the monarch migration in the spring. My students were thrilled with the scientists' report from Mexico before the migration began. When the scientists notified us that the spring migration had begun, my students began to post on a classroom map all the sightings as they were reported. With great excitement, we added our first observation of a monarch.

On-line, I discovered that the Entomology Department of the University of Kansas was actively recruiting classrooms to tag monarch butterflies for Monarch Watch (http://monarch.bio.ukans.edu). We purchased a $10 kit and began tagging the monarchs we had raised in bug boxes from caterpillars collected in the butterfly garden. The students had to report latitude, longitude, direction of flight, weather conditions, and sex of each released butterfly. In March, we received notification that one of our tagged butterflies had been recovered in El Rosario, Mexico, after having flown 1,365 miles. It was the first tagged monarch ever recovered in Mexico from Louisiana! My students were excited that they had contributed to a serious scientific study.

CHAPTER **6**

Opening School Doors to Parental Involvement

*S*chool doors are opening to parental involvement. Walk through the door of this chapter and take a closer look.

Chapter Overview

- **Addie Gaines**, a kindergarten teacher at Seneca Elementary School in Seneca, Missouri, explains the goals of her weekly newsletters.

- **William Fitzhugh**, a second-grade teacher at Reisterstown Elementary School in Reisterstown, Maryland, mentions three techniques he employs to maintain good home-school relationships.

- **Carla Becker**, a multiage classroom teacher for Grades 3, 4, and 5 at Norwalk Lab School in Norwalk, Iowa, shares her parental menu of opportunities.

- **Cindy Montonaro**, a kindergarten teacher at Huntington Elementary School in Brunswick, Ohio, shares one of her most popular classroom activities—"Doughnut Dilemma Day."

- **David V. Buus**, a second-grade teacher at Moorcroft Elementary School in Moorcroft, Wyoming, describes his "Exiting Report," which he uses to increase communications with his students and their parents.

- **Mary Bernard**, a third-grade teacher at Turtle Lake Elementary School in Shoreview, Minnesota, shares her parent/guardian communication ideas.

- **Pam Peters**, a kindergarten/first-grade teacher at Rossmoor Elementary School in Los Alamitos, California, says that parental involvement begins before the children ever enter the classroom. She explains meetings and conferences and shares her "Room 21 ABC List for Parents."

- **Patricia R. Bell**, a fourth-grade teacher at Shepardson Elementary School in Fort Collins, Colorado, explains her system of maintaining two-way (home-school) communication.

- **Sheri Radovich**, a third-grade teacher at Holladay Elementary School in Salt Lake City, Utah, explains her process of sending an envelope home with each student in her class to encourage communication.

- **Debbie Lerner**, a multiage classroom teacher (Grades 1, 2, and 3), says that one key to her planning each year is partnerships with citizens in the community who are actively working to create a healthier world.

- **Richard Morgan**, a music teacher at Beethoven Elementary School in Chicago, Illinois, discusses the importance of parents.

Weekly Newsletters

Addie Gaines
Seneca, Missouri

I find that a good way to keep parents interested and involved in their children's education is to send home weekly newsletters. I have done a weekly newsletter for 8 years and find that parents enjoy reading it and feel as if they are a part of what is going on at school. This may sound like a daunting task at first glance, but it is really quite manageable through the use of computer technology and a good desktop publishing program.

The goals for my newsletter are as follows:

1. To provide parents with the necessary insight and information about our classroom to engage their children in meaningful discussions about school.

2. To inform parents of our current learning objectives so that they can reinforce them at home.

3. To provide information about classroom and school events and to invite parents to participate when possible through sending needed supplies or volunteering and attending.

4. To provide positive reinforcement for the accomplishments of individual children and to express gratitude for parental involvement.

5. To share ideas with the other kindergarten teachers.

6. To communicate with the other special area teachers who work with my class and to encourage the integration of curriculum.

To expedite the process of publishing the weekly newsletter, "Inside Kindergarten," I save all the back issues in a file on my computer's hard drive. I design the masthead and format once a year; this both helps with the speed of publishing the letter and provides instant recognition of the newsletter for parents in the sea of documents that are sent home via backpacks each day. I also have set columns that appear each week.

The main column is devoted to our theme for the following week and details the objectives and activities related to that theme. It is intended to build interest and motivation for the new theme and to provide the parents with information about what their children will be working on. I also have a column that describes one "routine" class activity per week, along with the objectives for that activity and what the children will be learning.

Describing the daily schedule one segment at a time takes up one column per week for the first semester. Each month, the children of the month for our class are featured. I interview the children of the month and write a feature about each of them. I have a scanner attached to my computer, and I save a scanned school picture for each child and add it to the article. When individual children or groups of children have special accomplishments, I include them too. I will write about our all-star book-it readers when the time comes. This year, I wrote articles featuring our top PTO fund-raiser and the winner of the annual school ornament contest.

Each time we begin a new unit in mathematics, I describe the activities and objectives and relate them to the children's future mathematical learning. I also feature the new module in our alphabet/phonics learning sequence each time we start a new one. Other features include holiday plans, special projects, and assorted classroom happenings. I sometimes use the scanner to do a photomontage on the back of the newsletter and feature different events in class.

The photographs are by far the most popular item with the children. I provide copies of my newsletters to every child in my class, the other kindergarten teachers, the special area teachers, the principal, and the superintendent. This keeps everyone informed and involved with the happenings in our classroom.

Good Home-School Relationships

William Fitzhugh
Reisterstown, Maryland

1. A monthly newsletter is warmly received by parents. The newsletter gives information about skills their children will be learning in the coming month. It reviews the skills taught in the previous month and informs about the dates of upcoming class events and the supplies the children will be needing.

2. Parents are invited to have lunch with their child once a month in our classroom. Younger brothers and sisters, as well as grandparents, often come in for lunch, too. Informally, I meet and chat with parents about everyday life, not schoolwork. Parents get to know me as a person and as a parent with similar concerns.

3. At the beginning of the year, I send home a volunteer sheet with specific days and times that parents might want to volunteer in our

classroom on a regular basis. One parent comes in each day during our reading/language arts block to work one-on-one with children who need extra assistance. One parent volunteers to assist in our computer lab for our class.

Parental "Menu of Opportunities"

Carla Becker
Norwalk, Iowa

After 3 years of planning, visiting, reading, and researching, our new elementary Lab School opened. It was to be an alternative setting to the traditional elementary schools in our town of about 6,500. Student achievement is a major focus in our school, not unlike in most schools around the nation. Research shows a direct relationship between parental involvement and increased student achievement. With this in mind, the Lab School teachers developed a plan to increase parental involvement and make it one of our major goals.

In the early stages of the planning and development of our Lab School, an interested parent shared some powerful information with us. We were told that more parents would like to be involved but that they were intimidated by teachers. They felt uncomfortable and ignorant at school and were not sure how to become involved. In other words, parents felt "disinvited."

We teachers realized we would need to change the paradigm of "involvement" to accommodate working parents and the ways parents could become involved. Our original intent was to have some sort of contractual obligation for the parents to sign. After a discussion of this with a parent group, we changed our approach. What about providing opportunities that invited parents to become involved? Thus, our "Menu of Opportunities" evolved.

We brainstormed all the possible ways we could involve people in our school and in the education of the students. We tried to reach out not only to the parents but to the powerful resources in our surrounding areas as well. We tried to look at things from an entirely different perspective.

Menu of Opportunities

- Attend all conferences
- Attend potlucks
- Visit child(ren) at school
- Help with parties
- Help with field trips
- Provide transportation for field trips
- Act as parent presenter
- Be a parent shopper
- Make items at home
- Help with lunches
- Help with centers
- Organize events
- Help students with journaling
- Help students with story writing
- Serve on Parent Advisory Board
- Serve on specific committees
- Be a teacher's assistant at home
- Work with children at home
- Eat at school with your child(ren) once a year
- Type for the teachers

Please select at least three activities from the above list.

1. Attend all conferences

2. _____

3. _____

4. _____

Please return this to your child's teacher as soon as possible.

Parent's signature _____

When parents read with their children at home, they are involved. Shopping for school supplies on their own time is being involved. Sewing the eyes on puppets, cutting out letters, and writing names on folders are all ways parents have opportunities to participate in activities that involve the school and ultimately benefit the students. We found that the more parents did, the more they wanted to do. They became empowered and offered services and skills and materials before we asked or even recognized the need.

As teachers in traditional settings, we had always encouraged parents to become involved. The participation was usually limited to the customary homeroom mothers, field trip chaperons, parties, and the conventional manner we all had come to expect. What made it different? What had changed? We found several reasons to be true. First, we had underestimated our parents, their abilities, and their willingness to participate and become involved. We had unknowingly put parameters on the things they could do and the ways they could share in the education of their children.

We quite accidentally landed on a second and equally important reason: Our parents felt more comfortable being a part of our school setting. Our setting is open spaces by design. It has suited us and fits our needs quite nicely. Without the barriers of doors and walls, our parents have the freedom to walk in unannounced and with no disruption or distraction. It doesn't redirect any attention to the visitor, causing them any focus or embarrassment. They feel more at ease to walk in and observe or visit.

We also used these opportunities to have an extra pair of hands to help us. Every classroom has students who can benefit from having an adult listen to them read or help edit a story or go through a set of flash cards with them. There is a never-ending list of things that can be done. Many times, as we thought back to our previous experiences, it seemed as though when parents came to visit, they sat beside their child as silent observers. They did not partake and become actively involved in what was going on in the room. What a difference in our new setting with a new perspective!

We were eager to try something we had observed while visiting another school. We wanted to deviate from the normal in our lunch setting. We were eager to try serving lunch in a family-style environment. Our school does not have the luxury of an in-school lunchroom. Our students eat in their tables in their classrooms. The students are responsible for getting the milk, silverware, and plates for lunch. They put a tablecloth on the table, set the table, and get the bowls of food for the people in their group. They are responsible for the total cleanup after lunch. It is a pleasant atmosphere.

We stress restaurant manners and quiet voices. We encourage parents to come and eat with their children. The number of lunch guests is overwhelming. Away from the cafeteria environment, the noise, and the hubbub, parents and students find this to be a relaxing time to enjoy the company of others, share, and socialize. This was an added bonus to what we thought was an already positive experience.

We as educators make continuous and tremendous efforts to provide a safe, inviting atmosphere for all people who come through our doors. Our statistics boldly prove that we are providing an inviting atmosphere that has made parents feel welcome, needed, and an integral part of our whole school community. We let the families know this not only orally but also in newsletters and at our program at the end of the year where each family is given a certificate of recognition. They will always be important to us! We value and treasure their partnership in the education of "our" students. Everyone involved in our Lab School is living proof of the African proverb "It takes a whole village to raise a child."

I have no words of wisdom. What works for us may or may not work in your community or school. One thing I have learned will stay with me no matter where I go or where I teach: Never underestimate the power of a parent.

Doughnut Dilemma Day

Cindy Montonaro
Brunswick, Ohio

While learning the letter *O,* one of my kindergarteners' most popular classroom activities is "Doughnut Dilemma Day." On this day, various family members come to school to participate. I begin the activity by explaining what a dilemma is and giving a few examples of dilemmas and how I would go about solving them. At this point, each child and her or his family are given a paper plate with a buttermilk biscuit and an empty brown plastic prescription pill bottle. Everyone is instructed to use the bottle to cut a hole in the middle of the biscuit.

Each person visits a designated table where a room mother is frying doughnuts. The room mother gives everyone a fried doughnut, and each person sprinkles on powdered sugar, granulated sugar, or cinnamon and sugar. The doughnuts are then tied to strings of various lengths hanging from the ceiling. The dilemma is to eat a doughnut without using any hands!

Helpful Tips

To make this activity run smoothly, I do the following:

1. I teach two sessions of kindergarten a day, so I have afternoon room mothers come in the morning session to help fry and hang doughnuts. This allows my morning parents to enjoy the activity with their children and other family members. Then the morning room mothers return the favor so that afternoon room mothers can enjoy the activity with their children in the afternoon.

2. I have mother helpers fry some doughnuts a little ahead of time so that the children and adults aren't standing around waiting for frying to be done.

3. For a class of 28 children and approximately 50 family members, I use 16 to 20 cans of Pillsbury buttermilk biscuits (10 biscuits to a can).

▧ Daily Exiting Report

David V. Buus
Moorcroft, Wyoming

I used a particular teaching strategy for the first time this year, and it was successful. I wanted better communication with my children and their parents, so I devised a simple form I call the "exiting report." Each day, I fill out an exiting report for each child. The report has three sections: The first section is "What We Worked on Today." The second has a series of three faces: a smiley face, a so-so face, and a "not so good, very bad" frazzled face, with space provided to write an entry. The third section is "Special News."

At the beginning of the year, it took about 2 minutes to fill out a report for each child. Halfway through the year, I had the children brainstorm "What We Worked on Today" as I wrote it on the chalkboard. I had them copy our compilation of the day's activities from the chalkboard. Then I had each of the children color the face of their choice to reflect what kind of day they had at school and write a sentence explaining why they chose the particular face. The "Special News" section was for my special notes to parents and celebrations that individual children met on that given day. I chose one third of the class and personally wrote something positive about each of those children to their parents.

At first, it seemed overwhelming, but after a few weeks it became a daily routine. When the children could fill in the first two sections, it became about a 15-minute writing activity each day. The children then placed the exiting reports in their take-home folders. I received rave reviews from parents and administrators for the active communication between school and parents. It was also an excellent way for the children to reflect on their day at school.

This activity is only accomplished when I am present. The parents receive notice of this procedure on the first day of school.

Parent/Guardian Communication Ideas

Mary Bernard
Shoreview, Minnesota

1. *Communication Sheet:* This sheet goes home every day and is signed by a parent and returned each day. The students have a Turtle Lake folder to keep it in. I write a comment to two students per day about something positive they have done. Parents also write notes to me regarding a concern or just responding to a comment. I have 95% participation throughout the school year. On the back of each sheet, I print the spelling words for the week. They are very handy for the students to have to practice at home each day.

2. *Brown Bag Lunches:* I invite parents to bring brown bag lunches a few times a year and choose a topic to discuss about which the parents may have questions. This year, we discussed our new reading series.

The parents were thrilled with the discussion and felt more at ease with the new series.

3. *Good News Telephone:* The students have the opportunity to use the "Good News Telephone" when they accomplish special achievements. At this time, I call a parent at home or at work. For instance, parents are pleased to hear that their child received a 100% on a multiplication test or a Good Citizen Award.

4. *Good News Postcards:* I send these postcards to parents throughout the year to let them know how much I am enjoying their child, with examples of what their child has accomplished.

5. *Portfolio:* The students design fancy covers for their portfolios, and several pieces of their work are placed in these portfolios throughout the year. The students evaluate several pieces of work. As teacher, I evaluate some, as do parents. The portfolios are used at conferences to show the students' progress. I also use them at midterm. During this time, I send them home with questionnaires for the parents to fill out after they have evaluated their children's work.

In addition, I have developed a video portfolio in which I capture student presentations, special events, birthdays, and so on. By the end of the school year, each student has a 1-hour video portfolio of her or his learning experiences in third grade.

6. *Parent Information Night:* This event is held during the first week of school. I allow 1 hour to present information on my goals and my expectations of students and parents. I also explain what they can expect from me. This 1-hour session covers what a typical school day is like.

7. *Parents' Sharing Expertise:* I encourage and invite parents to share all skills pertinent to any area the class is studying. Doctors, geologists, lawyers, politicians, nurses, engineers, and businessmen have enriched our units of study.

8. *Et cetera Telephone Calls:* I make many telephone calls to discuss areas of concern, as well as to give positive feedback. Parents are encouraged and are always welcome to call me or to set up an appointment for a conference.

9. *Report Cards:* Report cards go out twice a year. The students receive O (Outstanding), S (Satisfactory), and N (Needs Improvement)

for personal development, as well as for academic achievement and effort. I make many written comments along with the grades.

10. *Conferences:* Conferences are held twice a year. The students are invited to be actively involved. We review goals and discuss progress, concerns, and achievements.

11. *Letters Home:* Every major project is explained in detail in a letter sent home well in advance of the project's due date. Parents sign on the communication sheet that they have received the letter and have reviewed it with their child.

Meetings and Conferences

Pam Peters
Los Alamitos, California

In my classroom, parental involvement begins before the children ever enter the classroom. The school holds a parent orientation for future kindergarten parents. At this time, I start to recruit any and all kinds of help. Below is a list of the types of volunteer help I enlist:

- Classroom volunteers (1 or 2 hours weekly)

- Field trip chaperons

- Printing parent (Many parents have access to various kinds of printing facilities, which alleviates problems arising from our limited budget for printing in our district.)

- Coloring, cutting, and pasting (Parents help make books or prepare projects.)

- Food donations for cooking

- Film developing

- Donations of various art materials: felt, ribbon, fabric, lace, pom poms, pipe cleaners, paper plates and cups, napkins, doilies, googly eyes, clothespins, feathers, buttons, pastas, beans and seeds, wood scraps, glues, glitters, etc.

On several occasions, parents are invited to the classroom. The first is the orientation. At that meeting, we as teachers tell the parents about all those little details they will need to know to make the first day and the first week of kindergarten successful for their child.

The second parent meeting is a Back-to-School Night. This is held in the evening, during the third week of school. Parents come without their children, and the teachers tell them about the curriculum and ways to help at home and answer questions.

The third parent occasion is called the Welcome Conference. This is a 30-minute conference held during the first month of school. Teachers meet with each family individually and devote the time to discussing what things about each child her or his teacher should know. We discuss health issues, personalities, interests, and strengths. Goals are set as a team for each child. This is a very positive meeting and sets the tone for teamwork for the rest of the year.

Then we have our progress conferences, which are held in November and March. We review report cards and show work samples. One of the biggest advantages about looping (staying with the same class for 2 or more years) is the notion of building "family." The parents really become allies, and the discipline problems diminish greatly!

In addition, I have developed a small home-school book each child carries back and forth daily. Parents can write to me, and I can write to them any time anyone has a question, concern, or something to praise or complain about. This keeps the parents involved on a daily basis. I do not write every day for every child, but it is there when needed.

Helpful Tips

I want to share my "Room 21 ABC List for Parents." I put each listed item up in the pocket chart at Back-to-School Night and discuss it. Because I am an ABC book collector, this is an understandable addition.

Parents who work full time and cannot volunteer during class hours are very happy to help out at home by cutting, coloring, printing, or donating, and their children receive the benefits of having involved families:

A is for art, artists

B is for books, butterflies, birthdays, butterfly of the week

C is for character education, conflict management, cooperative learning, computer

D is for dramatic play, diversity, donations

E is for earth science (also life and physical)

F is for friends, family, fun, field trips, French

G is for gifted children, guest speakers

H is for home fun, handwriting

I is for intellectual development, interests

J is for journal writing

K is for kitchen

L is for love, laughter, lunch, library books, looping

M is for music, mathematics

N is for numbers

O is for outside

P is for puppetry, poetry, phonemic awareness

Q is for quiet reading time

R is for rubber stamping, reading, recess, rules

S is for sign language, self-esteem, spelling, schedule, sharing

T is for talking

U is for us

V is for volunteers

W is for writing every day, Web page, Wacky Wednesday

X is for excellence

Y is for YOU

Z is for zoo

Two-Way Communication

Patricia R. Bell
Fort Collins, Colorado

During the early years of my teaching, I happened to work for a principal who thought I could do more to communicate with parents. At his suggestion, I began to write a weekly newsletter to parents. In that newsletter, I put information about what happened in class and what might be coming up. I put in parenting tips I gleaned from journals and other articles. I put in things about what the students had said and done in class. I left a space where I wrote a personal note to parents every week about their child.

Sometimes the personal note was about an accomplishment that week or about an area that was troublesome for the child. Sometimes the note might tell about a behavior problem and how I handled it. Once in a while, I might use the note to comment about something the child said or did that concerned or troubled me and I thought the parent could help.

This format served me well for several years, until I realized this was a one-way street of communication. The note was written on the newsletter, with other important information the families needed, and it did not return to school after the weekend. Parents were not encouraged to communicate with me. Additionally, I sometimes could not remember the comments. It was pointed out to me that some negative comments were not followed up with indicators of change or progress.

After pondering this observation for a summer, I decided to make a change. I set up a system using a folder for transporting student papers home, and in each folder I placed a brightly colored page with a note that the page should stay in the folder each week. I told parents that the newsletter would still go home but that the personal note would now be written on the colored page and they were invited to write back to me at any time.

This system has worked out very well for me for many years now. Some parents write regularly, others rarely. I now teach older students, and I notice a definite difference in the kinds of notes I write to parents and the notes they write back. Perhaps some of that is because the students read them, too. The older students use a daily planner, and although I designate a specific day for my writing to everyone (a day when

I have a planning period), parents write to me almost any time and rely on their children to call my attention to the notes. Likewise, I can jot a note on any day a special need comes up and expect it to be read when the parent signs off that the child has done nightly assignments.

I appreciate the encouragement the principal gave me to start this practice. The investment of time pays off in the progress students make and at conferences with parents. We know each other better by the time we sit down face-to-face, and many concerns have already been addressed.

Helpful Tips

My notes to parents often mention a subject or concept we worked on during the week and things they can do to strengthen, enrich, or reinforce them. Parents, in turn, will often comment about something their child has mentioned about an activity or something they have learned together.

Notes also comment on behavior problems that have come up, been handled, or still need follow-up. I often let parents know how I have handled a problem and what consequences have been evoked, and then I ask for their support and reinforcement. I have rarely found that parents are not supportive when the situation is explained to them.

Now, when our periodic report card conferences come around, the time is not spent on breaking new ground or explaining new developments. Rather, because of the notes, parents and I can sit down and talk about the progress their child is making, plan for further support in both academic and behavioral areas, and look to future developments. There are no surprises, and the parents, students, and I know that we have a good system of communication that we can continue to use.

▧ **Weekly Folders**

Sheri Radovich
Salt Lake City, Utah

I am a third-grade teacher of 20+ years and have an idea that works for elementary and middle grade teachers. Every week, I send home a folder (a 12 × 18-inch manila envelope) with each student in my class.

The folders are laminated with the students' names. Inside, I include tests, worksheets, creative writing, scored assignments, and the next week's spelling list. I staple notes about future assignments to alert the parents.

I also include a small (4 × 6-inch) form on colored paper, telling parents whether their child is missing any assignments for the week. I also have a place to check off whether the student's behavior for the week was satisfactory or needs improvement. Included is a place for parents' comments or questions and a place for the parents to sign. They send this back with the folder weekly, to be filled again the next week.

I usually send the folders home on Friday or Monday after school. Monday works better for me because the Friday before is a planning day and I organize and correct then. These folders have been received well by parents. I address the returned notes with comments by calling parents or writing notes to them with questions or concerns. I straighten out misunderstandings as soon as possible; it seems to avoid problems when conferences come around.

Being Good Neighbors

Debbie Lerner
Kansas City, Missouri

Schooling brings parents and teachers together in common purpose, and the best thing about it is that we both have the opportunity to make a difference in the ways we can help each student discover her or his uniqueness, develop it, and share it with others.

The teachers I admire most are professionals who build not only on technique but on tenderness. They reduce barriers between parents and themselves and create a safety in their relationships that makes communication and collaboration more possible on behalf of the students.

Since 1975, I have taught seven-, eight-, and nine-year-olds in a multiage classroom. Through a project-based curriculum, I try to develop confidence in my students by nurturing in them an understanding of the interrelationships between themselves and others. The idea of building community begins in our school, our neighborhoods, and then into the city at large.

My students know about being good neighbors because they live it through projects such as our "City Beautiful Awards" and the "Landmark Calendar" projects, which honor people in the community who are making a difference in the human-made environment.

They know it by working together with one another and with resources around them in real-life activities, such as our yearly collaboration with students in another school to celebrate Martin Luther King, Jr.'s birthday and Earth Day. These events include the collection of canned goods for our local food collection agency, a student-drawn poster created by the students and distributed citywide thanks to a local advertising agency that underwrites the project, and a parent support group, "The Dreamkeepers." A HEART FRIEND award to a member of the community is another feature of the event.

Each project throughout the year is designed to expose students to a broad range of skills. They are helped to develop verbal and visual communication skills and to learn about a range of careers and lifestyles. They are exposed to social as well as environmental issues. Students learn prosocial values as we study the community and its citizens; skills of patience, responsibility, and effort are also acquired in the process of completing these projects.

I truly believe that it is important to work with the community, that the community is no stronger than the educational systems within it, and that the challenge is to learn the art of true cooperation. Partnerships with our community's citizens who are actively working to create a healthier world is a key to my planning each year.

For further details about our classroom projects, look for the special feature "Walk Around the Block: My Home, My School, My City" in the November/December 1996 issue of *Social Studies and the Young Learner.*

Importance of Parents

Richard Morgan
Chicago, Illinois

All children can learn regardless of their socioeconomic status. If we as parents and educators invest quality time in our children's learning, it will ensure a valued education.

Children should feel good about education. We can help accomplish this by taking a more active role. Parents must understand that schools share the same goals. Parents should also understand that their advice and participation are important. They know their children better than anyone else. Parents should periodically schedule teacher conferences at a time that is convenient to discuss homework, study habits, conduct, and so on.

Parents can review homework together with their children and help them prepare for the next school day. Parents should also be able to admit when they don't understand something.

Parents are a child's most important influence. Parents must therefore strive to be positive influences. Parents' attitudes and actions influence their child at home and school. As parents and educators, we have to understand that our children are individuals and that, therefore, we should allow them to express their thoughts and ideas to us so that we may set reliable goals and plan how to achieve them.

I am a firm believer that a person should not measure success on the basis of what someone else has accomplished, but rather on the goals that person has set for her- or himself. Too often, we as parents and educators want our children to travel the same road we took in reaching our goals, and in contrast we avoid those challenges we fought so hard to conquer. Children will perform much better when they know that parents and teachers are standing at their side to support them.

CHAPTER 7

Integrating Inclusion in the Classroom

*T*his chapter discusses inclusion in the classroom.

Chapter Overview

- **Stacy Kasse**, a fifth-grade teacher at Taunton Forge School in Medford, New Jersey, shares her Dr. Martin Luther King, Jr. project, which works well with inclusion students.

- **Carla Becker**, a multiage classroom teacher (Grades 3, 4, and 5) at Norwalk Lab School in Norwalk, Iowa, believes that community building is the key to making inclusion work. She explains how inclusion works in her classroom.

- **Patricia R. Bell**, a fourth-grade teacher at Shepardson Elementary School in Fort Collins, Colorado, discusses teaching in a full inclusion school. She says that families of special needs students request to come to her school.

- **Rachel Ely**, an elementary art specialist at McGavock Elementary School in Nashville, Tennessee, discusses inclusion in the visual arts classroom. She says that communication is the key to creating a least restrictive environment for all students in the visual arts classroom.

➡ **Rosemary Johnson**, a fifth-grade teacher at Valley View Elementary School in Rapid City, South Dakota, works in conjunction with the learning center. The learning center model for its special education students has inclusion at its base.

Dr. Martin Luther King, Jr. Project

Stacy Kasse
Medford, New Jersey

It's the day back from winter break, and my class of fifth graders at Taunton Forge School are hard at work. Every book about Dr. Martin Luther King, Jr., is on our fireplace hearth. (The hearth is a fake but a great classroom tool.) The students start to read and research everything they can about Dr. King. Those who go on the Internet do some "surfing" and find some wonderful sites from MLK and Civil Rights links.

The second day back, the students write, in class, a persuasive letter to me, explaining why they should be allowed to work in the group of their choice. These groups are drama, art, poetry, and music. I remind them that the written word is very powerful, and they all try to do their best, keeping in mind spelling, punctuation, and grammar.

Once I read the letters and make "a teacherlike decision" about groups (I'm cautious, not foolish, about my groups), I send a letter home to parents explaining the project. The students have 1 day to brainstorm in their groups about what they want to accomplish. A typical presentation includes the following: *drama*—write and perform a short play about the life and times of Dr. King; *music*—compose words and music to a song about Dr. King and be prepared to perform it; *poetry*—write 5 to 10 different types of poems about Dr. King and be prepared to present these poems during the presentation; and *art*—using different media, draw three different events that happened in Dr. King's life.

You may decide whether your students can work together as a group or individually. This gives everyone a choice and covers all aspects of multi-intelligence. I find that the drama group probably needs the most supervision. I make sure they are making a list of important events. Then they may break off into smaller groups so that each can write a scene. I look over all the scenes, type them up, and then, if I must, choose people for the roles. This doesn't happen very often, but sometimes I have many good actors and no directors; this is where I do my job as the adult.

I give the students about a week to practice, write, draw, and sing or play instruments. This is not a time to be squeamish about noise: In one corner, someone might be playing a keyboard; in another corner, someone might be working with oils at an easel; poets may be reciting their poems; and the actors might be working on volume and expression. Watching the students do what they love to do is one of the best times in my classroom.

On the day of the performance, our classroom is crowded with video cameras, parents, and students from each grade level. (We have the teachers sign up for the times they want to bring their classes.) By the time the students perform for the fourth time, they are really into it. When I hear the "I Have a Dream" speech and listen to the students sing "Martin" and "Heroes" by Jonathon Sprout, I know that all the hard work is worth every moment. And to top it off, one of our students' drawings was entered in a statewide art contest. Never say "no" to your dream. Dr. King wouldn't have.

Helpful Tips

Inclusion idea? Absolutely. The Dr. Martin Luther King, Jr. project works well with inclusion students. The special education teacher will know exactly how to group students. Ask the special education teacher to go from group to group, modifying or helping out inclusion students.

▨ Making Inclusion Work

Carla Becker
Norwalk, Iowa

Being a product of the 1970s, I began my teaching career in the "perfect" classroom. The students in my room were the ones capable of acquiring their academic skills in the customary learning style. This was something I had certainly been educated to accomplish. No special needs students were in my class. They went to "the room down the hall" with the special education teacher. I never knew exactly what the teacher did in "that" room with "those" students. I was sure, however, that she possessed skills and abilities that had never even been introduced to me. Of course, there was integration; "those students" were with the rest of the class for the necessities like, PE, music, lunch, and recess. But for some reason, "those students" did not feel a part of the class. They felt singled out and isolated. We, the educated ones, couldn't imagine what was wrong.

Things slowly changed. Our district mandated that "those students" be integrated for everything except reading, writing, and mathematics. So, there sat "those students," many unable to read and write, in the middle of social studies and science class.

Finally, about 6 or 7 years ago, my district made very dramatic and innovative changes in the area of special education. Our school became a paradigm pioneer in meeting the needs of our special education students. The special education director believed two things: (a) our current special education program was not very successful in teaching students the skills they needed, and (b) a teacher is a teacher. These are basic beliefs, but ones that sent special education into a spin.

Why did we isolate "those students"? How did we expect their social skills to improve or change when many times their only models were inappropriate ones? Whatever made us believe that special education teachers possessed magical skills in dealing with students? Oh, sure, they have teaching strategies that regular education teachers perhaps weren't taught but certainly had the capabilities of successfully acquiring.

Our collaborative model was set up in the following manner: With six sections per grade level, two sections were identified as the collaborative rooms. Teacher participation was strictly voluntary. Students identified as having special needs were split between these two rooms. A resource teacher was then assigned to collaborate in the teaching of the students in these rooms. Another contributing fact was cooperative learning. All the teachers in our district had been trained in the Johnson and Johnson cooperative learning model.

We tried as best we could to group each classroom heterogeneously, with equal numbers of students functioning at the high, middle, and low areas to accommodate this strategy. So, in the collaborative rooms, special needs students filled these spaces.

I volunteered to be involved in this new initiative. I remembered a poem hanging on a wall in my mother's home—"Children Learn What They Live." I believe that children must be treated with respect in order to show respect. This is not an intrinsic skill. Children deserve to be listened to and to have their dignity preserved.

In this constantly changing world, teachers must learn to be facilitators of learning, not merely dispensers of knowledge. This led me to the realization that all my students needed to be more actively involved in their learning, not only age-appropriate but also individually appropriate. It is imperative that curriculum content, materials, activities, and methodologies be proportionate with a child's level of development and level of readiness.

Being a regular classroom teacher in my collaborative setting and teaming with a special education teacher gave me a new insight into the ability to meet the needs of all my students. The inclusion of my special education students gave them the opportunity to receive their primary instruction within the least restrictive environment.

We spend an enormous amount of time discussing some fundamentals of life in our classroom. We all have strengths as well as weaknesses. We all are good at some things and do them very well. And we all are not very good at other things and need help to do or improve. I use myself as an example. I was always a very good reader and speller. My classmates would come to me for help in those areas. But when it came to the mathematical/logical domain, I was the one seeking help and advice.

My class and I go around the circle and share some things we consider our strengths. All answers are accepted. The students follow my cues. I treat everyone with dignity and respect. All strengths and abilities are celebrated. We recognize that all areas of strength and things we think we do well may not fall into an academic category. We discuss people like the one little girl in my room several years earlier. She couldn't read, write, or work mathematically without a lot of help and modifications. However, she was known as "The Organizer." She always listened to the directions. She knew when things were due, how they were to be done, and all the other necessary information. What a valuable group member!

The multiple intelligences are studied and discussed in depth. In our school, it's not how smart are you, but how are you smart. We take surveys and mark our strongest intelligence. We share where we use our strengths and how we might help others by using those aptitudes. People who are good builders have the opportunity to show their skills at the construction center or the building center with blocks, marbleworks, or Legos. Naturalists can find their niche at the discovery center or the animal center.

We created our learning centers to fit the multiple intelligences. We were limited by our own creativity, imaginations, and of course the dreaded one, our budget. We constructed about 17 centers, using things we had on hand, such as puzzles, stamps, and a keyboard, and used our monies for things we lacked and could afford. We diligently worked to make sure there was something for everyone.

Community building is the key to making inclusion work. The time I spend initially makes all the difference in the world in whether or not my students are accepting and tolerant of one another. We dialogue about doing one's best and putting forth our greatest efforts. We all agree that if we do that and continue to try to improve, no one can ask more of us.

I let my students know immediately that I have many weaknesses and that I make numerous mistakes. I might as well be honest with them because they will find it out on their own soon enough! I find that my students will accept my shortcomings and are more than willing to help me with them if I am honest. Children are so smart. They can spot a phony a mile away. They can embrace the fact that I made a mistake or that I simply just don't know something. But, they can spy a coverup faster than the media. Don't try to tell them it was meant to be that way! My students recognize my weaknesses of disorganization and lack of memory. They know I rely on them in many ways to help me with these things, and they never let me down.

One of the first things we do every day is have a class meeting. We go over our agenda for the day and discuss any schedule changes or special happenings. Sometimes we talk about current events. This is also a time we just talk. We can discuss any topic. At this time, I bring to their attention the subject of joking and teasing. Feelings of rejection, isolation, and humiliation are ones everyone can relate to. No one is immune to these unwanted emotions. We outline the parameters for jokes and teasing. If someone's feelings get hurt or someone is physically hurt, then it's not a joke. We discuss the difference between laughing at someone and laughing with someone. If someone is not laughing along, then it more than likely was not an appropriate joke.

If I expect a behavior, then I must teach it and make sure we have opportunities to practice it. We give examples of what it does or does not look like or sound like. I do not automatically assume that we all have the same foundation of understanding in the beginning. We all come from very different backgrounds, homes, families, and expectations.

Social skills are an important part of what we do. Social skills include personal relationships, decision making, and conflict resolution. If the expectations are clearly defined and jointly determined by the students and myself, then our community of learners is constantly being developed. Team building is an ongoing process. The power of this community centers around the involvement and ownership in which my students have been invited and encouraged to participate.

When labels are abolished, students with special needs benefit by acquiring increased self-esteem, improved social skills, and stronger academic skills. My regular education students gain skills beyond measure. These include having greater respect and tolerance for individual differences, valuing oneself and others, and being aware of and celebrating the diversity among all of us. One cannot put a price on these rewards that reach beyond the classroom walls and make a powerful difference in the lives of all children.

Teaching is a God-given gift. In turn, our students are gifts given to us, each uniquely wrapped. Each one is special, no one more than the other, waiting to be opened and discovered, cherished and nurtured. We as teachers are given the ability to reach out and touch all children to help them realize their own unique potential.

A Way of Life

Patricia R. Bell
Fort Collins, Colorado

From the first day I came to Shepardson Elementary School to teach more than 20 years ago, I began to work with special needs students. Our school was new then and specially designed to accommodate children in wheelchairs. Since then, we have seen children who use walkers, had to be prone all day, require a multitude of special communication devices, and just about any other situation you can imagine that qualifies them for special education considerations.

From the beginning, the goal of the staff was to include these special needs students in as much of the school day and activities as possible. But for a time, they continued to have a room of their own and were not included on class rosters. Teachers with special education certificates were also housed in those separate rooms and were guests in the regular classrooms.

After some years spent in this model, some of us began to want to expand to a more orchestrated and team approach. We wanted to serve all students with special needs in the regular classroom. We wanted to stop pulling out students as much as we could. We read and talked about what full inclusion would mean for us and for all the students. Parents of special education students expressed their desire that we move in that direction as well. I was most moved and influenced by hearing a teacher colleague talk about her own special needs daughter and the dreams and hopes they both held. She talked about the civil rights of her child, and that really hit home for me.

Thus, it came to pass that our school became a full inclusion school when we opened our doors in the autumn of 1990. We have never looked back, but it has not been without struggle. We did away with separate special education rooms, and every student's name appeared on a class roster. Our special education teachers moved their desks to locations closer to classrooms and set their schedules to work in classrooms. We looked for ways to work together and to serve all students.

Many teachers have asked for more training to feel more comfortable in this setting. Some teachers have found that this situation is not appropriate for them. But those of us who continue to work at Shepardson have seen many good things happen through the years.

Our school has become known in the district for this program, and we have seen families move into our area to be able to attend here. Families of special needs students also request to come to our school. Balancing the needs of all our students has become a major concern each year as we allocate staffing and other resources.

We would not go back to a format that separates and compartmentalizes our students. We have all benefited from the variety of experiences that have come our way. Perhaps we learned some sign language in our class because it helped us communicate with a special student and made that student feel accepted, or perhaps we all learned to use and share some new technological device that allowed a student to produce work in the classroom. Perhaps classmates recognized that someone else learned in a different way or took a bit more time or had a different area of expertise. Benefits certainly accrued every time a teacher examined a task or assignment and thought about how best to present it so that all students would understand. Inclusion is now a way of life for us, and like life, there are always new things to learn and experience.

Helpful Tips

Having students with special needs can be rewarding as well as challenging. You have to get to know both the student and his or her family to understand them well. Be sure to ask what the parents hope to have their child accomplish during the time in your classroom. Often, their words will help you focus on goals that are the most realistic for the child.

One year, I had a student whom the other students had a hard time interacting with and who did not feel a part of the class. Her behaviors were difficult for the others to understand, and thus it seemed difficult for them to see her as a member of the class. She could keep up with them academically in some areas, but her social and developmental skills were behind those of the class. Another staff member offered to come into the class and show pictures and tell about her own special needs daughter while I took that one student and did something outside class with her. From that day on, it seemed to me that the class had a better understanding of how to approach, help, and befriend the student. Perhaps they were able to say and ask things when we were out of the room that they had not been able to previously. I am indebted to that teacher for being so willing to share her own personal story and that of her daughter.

Inclusion in the Visual Arts Classroom

Rachel Ely
Nashville, Tennessee

An elementary art specialist has the challenge and opportunity of teaching art to all students. The visual arts are for all students. The instructor's pursuit of the necessary modifications and interventions is a continuous search. A "regular" classroom that may include autistic, hearing impaired, deaf, and visually impaired, as well as gifted and talented students calls for creative methods of teaching.

Communication is the key to creating a least restrictive environment for all students in the visual arts classroom. By communicating with parents, students, "regular" and special education teachers, and the appropriate specialists about goals and expectations, the art specialist can comprehend and implement appropriate strategies to assist the special needs student. Observing in the regular and special education classrooms and participating in multidisciplinary team meetings, where individual education plans are developed, assist the art specialist in creating an atmosphere conducive to learning. For included or mainstreamed students, the visual arts often become the most comfortable means of communication. All students of all capabilities benefit from the arts.

When the communication skills of one or more special education students shut down in a mainstreamed or included environment, the art specialist should consider a different setting for that student or group of students. For example, if a group of autistic students benefits more from the teaching of life skills through crafts than from a more formal visual arts course, then create a life-skills crafts course. Projects such as sewing, weaving, and latch hook empower autistic students to succeed in crafts while learning life skills and finding comfort in repetition.

If the success of deaf or hearing impaired students is dependent on the instructor, then take sign language courses to communicate with those students. Practice signs before the art lessons with the deaf students, and demand the attention of their minds and their eyes. The sign vocabulary learned in the art room should be age appropriate and relevant to the lessons. If learning sign language is not an option for the art specialist, then request an interpreter in the classroom at all times.

Demanding the attention of students' minds is not a new concept, but the avenues through which to engage a blind student's mind are sometimes foreign to visual arts instructors. Opportunities to teach art to the blind are challenging and rare, and the definitions of success in art are varied when a student's vision is impaired. Lessons that incorporate texture are essential when teaching the blind, and the use of the sense of smell comes in handy when teaching colors. When teaching color to a blind or visually impaired student, introduce color as a scent, relating the colors to fruits—for example, red = cherry, yellow = lemon, orange = orange, and blue = blueberries. If students can recognize the scent of a specific fruit, then they can independently choose scented colored markers for their drawings. The sense of taste may also be used to reinforce a blind student's memory of color through scent and taste.

Modifications and interventions are part of teaching in the visual arts. As for the "regular" and the gifted and talented students, art is designed to encompass different levels of abilities. On an elementary level, gifted and talented students may be challenged simply by the instructor's mentioning a more complex idea. Every lesson should be challenging to all students in the visual arts classroom because problem-solving and thinking skills are used in every lesson that meets the National Standards of the Visual Arts. All students regardless of ability levels will benefit from appropriate modifications and interventions by the art specialist.

Incorporating Inclusion in the Classroom

Rosemary Johnson
Rapid City, South Dakota

Schools in the Rapid City area have adopted the learning center model for special education students. This model works with inclusion at its base. The Learning Center is more than a room in our school. It is a way of teaching students who have special needs. It also helps with the borderline students who do not qualify for special education but need some extra assistance to be successful.

Valley View is one of 18 elementary schools in the Rapid City School District. It is a small school of about 280 students, with two sections of each grade, kindergarten through Grade 5. The school services a low socioeconomic area of town and has many students from one-parent families. These factors add to the difficulty students must overcome to be successful at school. For many students, success at school is just not high in importance. They are trying to satisfy their basic needs of food, shelter, and safety.

When special education students are placed in my classroom, I attempt to meet their needs within the regular classroom as much as possible. To do this, I need to work in conjunction with the Learning Center.

The Learning Center special educator and I work together to meet the goals and objectives on each student's individualized education plan (IEP).

We use several strategies to keep the students in the regular classroom as much of the day as possible. One strategy used in our school is to have an instructional assistant with the student in the classroom when needed. This allows the student to be in the classroom and benefit from the experience. When that is not possible, we try to have the student do either a reduced assignment or a parallel assignment related to the material taught.

One year, I had a special education student who had fragile X syndrome. This involves mental retardation especially in language skills. This student could not function all day in the regular classroom, but he could manage short periods in the regular classroom. We came up with a schedule that worked for him: He was in the classroom for all classroom routines and special area classes, and he also stayed in the classroom during science and social studies. When the class was doing something I could not alter for him, I would conference with the Learning Center special educator, and we would have an alternate activity for him.

I have a special education student this year who reads at a preprimer level. She understands material presented to her orally, but she cannot read it on her own. Strategies that have worked for her include peer assistance, Learning Center aide, reduced assignments, and teacher-read tests. This student is in the regular classroom most of the day. She is pulled out for special reading instruction but remains for everything else.

I believe that all students can be in class with their peers at least some of the day. It takes some time and planning on the part of everyone concerned, but I believe that it is worthwhile for everyone.

CHAPTER **8**

Teaching Social Studies in the Elementary Grades

*H*ere are two social studies lessons.

▧ Chapter Overview

- ➡ **Maggie Lee Costa**, a career education coordinator at the Stanislaus County Office of Education in Modesto, California, shares "Understanding Justice," a lesson giving students the opportunity to understand discrimination.

- ➡ **Barbara McLean**, a library media specialist at Joshua Eaton Elementary School in Reading, Massachusetts, shares "Traveling Pals," a schoolwide activity using stuffed animals to experience travel to foreign lands and areas of the United States.

📓 Understanding Justice

Maggie Lee Costa
Modesto, California

Age Range: K-8

Step 1

Come into the room with your eyes full of excitement. Give off a signal that something "big" has occurred. At an appropriate time, announce that you have a very important piece of information to share. Get your students' attention.

Say, "Class, I have some very important news. I have just come from a meeting with your principal. You know that I think you are a great class in terms of responsibility and attitude, and apparently others have noticed too. So, here is what is going on . . ."

Go to the chalkboard and write a series of delicious rewards that your group decides. Make the rewards something quite possible and extremely appealing. Students really get into this. Be sure to use the following phrase for each of the four or five rewards: "All the students in Room _____ will . . ." I used such things as ". . . will have 5 extra minutes of morning recess per day from now until the end of the year"; ". . . will be treated to art classes three mornings per week"; ". . . will be invited for a free dinner at The Red Lobster (They LOVE this! The roof nearly came down when I said this yesterday!); and ". . . will be invited to an extra field trip in June" (a cookout and swim party at the teacher's home). They are so invested in the joy of this that they can hardly contain themselves. Keep adding comments like, "You deserve it! I am so glad the principal noticed your good behavior because you are all entitled to a reward like this!" You have to be good at acting for this to have an impact.

Step 2

Students will invariably ask whether this is real. This is your signal to hesitate a bit and then say, "Well, as a matter of fact, I'm glad you asked." Tell them again, it IS real (act, act, act), but saunter over to the chalkboard and casually erase the words "All the students" in the first sentence. Say, "There is this one change." Then replace the erased words with "The girls." Do this for each one of the rewards.

Step 3

Depending on your class, there may be stunned silence or you may have caused a riot. Ask, "So, you don't think this is fair?" "NO!!!" they will shout. Agree with that. Say, "You're right. I agree. Let's take a vote. We'll vote on each of these rewards." At this point, they are slightly mollified, but still they realize that something is out of kilter. Then you add the final zinger: "Oh, yes. By the way, only the GIRLS can vote." "WHAT???!!" they will grouse. "Yes." Reiterate and then take the vote. Very few girls will vote.

Comments about fairness, rightness, and inclusion/rejection are guaranteed to follow. Guide this discussion carefully so that you can help the students truly internalize the concepts of voting rights, discrimination, and equality, the very issues at the heart of Dr. Martin Luther King, Jr.'s work. Make analogies all over the place. One 8-year-old girl said, "This isn't right because we are all in this class." I agreed and used her comment to illustrate that we are all in a democracy— equally endowed with certain rights. Remember to include the fact that people from all races and religions and walks of life participated in this struggle, just as the girls did who did not want to vote were showing their solidarity with the poor boys who were left out of all the treats.

Step 4

Wrap up the lesson by confessing that you played a trick on them. Tell them they will never forget this lesson because they have now experienced true discrimination in a way that helps them realize the terrible situation that faced people of color in this country and that Dr. Martin Luther King, Jr.'s work made a tremendous impact. We know this because of the evident changes. I am very open with the class about the need to continue the vigil for kindness and justice, today and in the future, so that this country and the world can continue to improve.

It has been my experience that this lesson is a powerful and successful tool for educating young people and for equipping them with a true sense of Dr. Martin Luther King, Jr., and the civil rights movement he inspired.

 **Traveling Pals**

Barbara McLean
Reading, Massachusetts

OVERVIEW

This schoolwide activity uses small stuffed animals to help students experience travel to other areas of the United States and to foreign lands. By tracking our pals on their adventures through photographs and postcards, these travels become more meaningful and attractive to the entire school community.

CONNECTION TO THE CURRICULUM

Geography, history, economics, global studies, mathematics, language arts, art, music

CONNECTION TO THE NATIONAL GEOGRAPHY STANDARDS

Standard 1: How to use maps and other geographic tools

Standard 4: The physical and human characteristics of place

GRADE RANGE

K-8

THEMES

Location, place, region

TIME

Each class is introduced to "Traveling Pals" at the beginning of the school year for approximately 15 minutes. Follow-up takes place in classrooms throughout the year as pals return with interesting artifacts from their travels. An introduction is given in the first PTO newsletter each year to let new families learn about this ongoing program.

MATERIALS

Small stuffed animals

Small library Hang up Plastic Bags, 8 1/2 × 10-inches (Style #3, Item #L61-79233, Highsmith Company 1-800-558-2110)

Mock passports

Permanent markers, identification tags

U.S. and world maps, push pins

Blank world map to use for display (Hammett Company, 1-800-333-4600, Giant Map [48 × 72-inches], code 87106 7877; made of corrugated cardboard)

OBJECTIVES

1. Use postcards and photographs to read the landscape of location

2. Identify leisure activities and relate to physical characteristics of place

3. Research country and its culture

4. Develop schoolwide activity encouraging geography awareness, family participation, and creativity

SUGGESTED PROCEDURES

1. Purchase small stuffed animals (The number of pals depends on the size of the school.)

2. Students select names for each traveling pal.

3. Develop a travel bag and passport for each pal (Write all the information on the front of a plastic travel bag with a permanent marker.) We change bags a few times a year. Passports travel along with the animals on trips. (These have been stamped by customs officials in many countries.)

4. Explain the procedures for signing out pals. Discuss the lobby display and how to track the pals. (I ask for a note from a parent who requests a pal with dates of travel. This helps us keep track of when pals are available to travel again.) We sign out pals on a first-come basis unless this is a first-time family or new destination, which is given priority.) We require each family to bring back a photograph of our pal on location or a postcard showing location. These postcards/photographs become the display.

5. Alert parents of the availability of pals through the PTO newsletter and update.

6. Send a press release to the local newspaper, announcing the program to the community. Tie it into the school goal of geographic/ global understanding.

7. Invite as guest speakers any adults who have traveled with our pals.

8. Set up a travel schedule. This is a sign-up in the library.

EXTENDING THE LESSON

Have students research a country, state, or tourist attraction by using materials brought by returning travelers.

Have students create a travel brochure highlighting sights visited by pals.

Have each family write a journal of the adventures of both the family and their pal while traveling.

Determine time zones and miles traveled to destination. Keep a total for each pal.

Have each student fill out a form telling about the trip.

ASSESSMENT

The informal program assessment is based on inquiries, photographs/postcards returned, journals, and interest from students and parents.

CHAPTER **9**

Celebrating Art and Music

*T*his chapter looks at art and music in the curriculum.

Chapter Overview

- **Larry Hewett**, an elementary art instructor at Chadbourn Elementary School in Chadbourn, North Carolina, discusses five parts to integration of the arts at his school. This includes the Adopt-a-Star Program and the Kids Are Authors, Too Program.

- **Susan Gabbard**, a visual arts teacher at Nichols Hills Elementary School in Oklahoma City, Oklahoma, explains how to teach four steps of art criticism.

- **Barry K. Elmore**, a music specialist in Chicago, Illinois, uses rhythm to call the class to order and as a foundation for music instruction.

- **Fred Koch**, a K-3 music specialist at Deer Path Elementary School and Cherokee School in Lake Forest, Illinois, says that at the primary level, one of the easiest and most powerful ways to integrate music is through language arts experiences with the use of songs. He explains how to make music come alive in the classroom.

155

Integrating the Arts

Larry Hewett
Chadbourn, North Carolina

Integration of the arts at Chadbourn Elementary School consists basically of five parts:

Part 1: Working Collaboratively With Classroom Teachers

Working with classroom teachers enables me to reinforce what students are studying in the classroom. And yes, on occasion, classroom teachers also reinforce what I am working on in the art room.

Integration of the arts needs to work both ways. With the education of the student in mind, we develop strategies and lesson plans that will help each other and at the same time allow us to cover our individual competencies and goals. Along with teaching the basics of art with students, we also discuss science, grammar, mathematics, social studies, geography, health, and other content areas. The classroom teachers and I have a good rapport with one another.

I am constantly keeping abreast of what students will be studying in the weeks ahead so that I will be able to plan a lesson to compliment what they're doing in the classroom. If the first-grade teachers are discussing insects, we do a project about insects. We might even read Eric Carle's book *The Very Hungry Caterpillar* in the art room for motivation. If weather is being taught in second grade, we would probably do a painting about thunderstorms, clouds, snow, tornadoes, and so on. If my fourth graders are studying Blackbeard the pirate as part of North Carolina history, we would do research about his physical appearance. Then, after sharing our information with each other, the students would do oil pastel portraits of the notorious villain.

And I can't forget November, Indian Heritage Month, and February, Black History Month. We always do integrated projects during these months, as well as study various Native American and black artists and their artwork. In all these projects, I am able to cover my art objectives as prescribed by the North Carolina Standard Course of Study, as well as reinforce the curricula of the classroom teachers. I simply use whatever they're teaching as the subjects or themes for my projects.

Part 2: Entering Contests or Competitions

I like to enter students in contests or competitions that I might use as a schoolwide theme. The best example of this is when I entered our school in a national contest called "Murals Reflecting Prevention." The theme was drug, alcohol, and tobacco abuse and how to prevent it. While we worked on this mural for a week, all the teachers integrated this same theme into their curricula. It was a wonderful experience for all of us, and we were very fortunate in being chosen to represent North Carolina in an exhibit in the Capitol in Washington, D.C. Our mural was also chosen as one of 12 to be printed in a calendar that was distributed nationwide.

Part 3: Using the Adopt-a-Star Program

The Adopt-a-Star Program is a program I started 5 years ago in which our school adopts nationally known artists and authors. A large percentage of our students are deprived in many ways—especially culturally. Some probably will never leave North Carolina during their lifetimes. For too many of them, their lives are confined to the boundaries of Columbus County. I've always said that I can't take my students out into the world, but with the help of Adopt-a-Star, national and foreign art exchanges, and the Internet, I can bring the world to them here in Chadbourn Elementary School. So far, we have adopted 45 nationally and internationally known artists. Just last week, I sent an e-mail to our possible 46th adoptee. Once agreeing to be our adoptee, the artist sends biographical information plus any other material he or she might have available that I can use as resource material for my students. During the last 5 years, I have acquired visual aids that I never would have been able to purchase because of my limited art budget. Artists have sent such things as autographed posters and prints, magazine articles, gallery brochures, photographs, videos, T-shirts, sketch books, note cards, and dolls.

After I review all the material, I develop a lesson plan introducing the adoptees to my students. The lesson usually pertains to the medium the adoptee uses or to his or her subject matter. While working on these projects, I'm either videotaping or photographing my students. On completion, I send the artists samples of my students' work, photographs or a video, plus student letters of appreciation. The results have been amazing.

These artists are also integrated into my curriculum, as well as into those of the classroom teachers. (For example, R. C. Gorman was one of my first Native American adoptees. My students studied his artwork during November, Indian Heritage Month. Another artist, Robert Wyland, creator of the "Whaling Walls," was introduced to my first graders while they were studying ocean life.) Each year, we adopt approximately 5 to 10 artists. We adopt artists who are African American, Native American, white, and of Spanish descent, their ages ranging from 13 to 95.

Each artist sends my students a letter that I frame and hang in the art room. We have been very fortunate to have two of these artists actually visit our school for a whole day. Tarleton Blackwell, from Manning, South Carolina, and Tony Ryals, from Jacksonville, Florida, have both visited our campus. During their visits, we had schoolwide celebrations for them in which we decorated our school with hogs for Tarleton and smiley faces and turtles for Tony.

Part 4: Using the A.R.T.S.—Our Advancing Relations Through Sharing Program

Each year, I do at least two art exchanges. One is with another elementary school somewhere in the United States; the other is an international exchange. In my 6 years at Chadbourn Elementary School, our students have exhibited their artwork in approximately 50 cities in 25 states, as well as in 8 foreign countries, Ireland, Japan, Australia, Israel, Bermuda, and African countries. When we do a national or foreign art exchange, classroom teachers gladly take part in discussing these states and countries.

The foreign exchanges are wonderful ways in which different customs, cultures, beliefs, and ways of life can be introduced to students. This is also a wonderful time to go to a map or globe and start teaching geography. Letter writing is also used quite a bit when we do our exchanges.

Part 5: Using the Kids Are Authors, Too Program

Two years ago, I applied for a Bright Ideas grant from Brunswick Electric Membership Cooperative, one of our local utility companies. We were very fortunate in receiving a $1,000 grant that financed the purchase of 25 Illustory kits (ordered from Chimeric, P. O. Box 101149, Denver CO 80250-1149; check with Learningsmith for availability). The fourth-grade teachers selected five original stories written by their students. These stories were edited and divided into pages in the classrooms. Then, in the art room, we divided into teams and worked cooperatively to illustrate these stories. It took us about 7 or 8 weeks to sketch out ideas, do finished pencil renderings, and then color illustrations by using markers.

Once completed, the kits were mailed back to the company; a few months later, we received hardbound books of our work. The students were able to purchase copies of these books, and the originals were donated to our library. This project was an overwhelming success. We did it again the following year without the aid of a grant. Our teachers and principal realized this was a wonderfully integrated project. It truly is integration at its best. This year, with the help of a Festival for Youth grant from the Milken Family Foundation, we were able to include our third graders in the project as well.

Helpful Tips

When working collaboratively on integrated lessons, you must allow an appropriate amount of time for planning. I like to have several weeks for planning each integrated lesson, but it doesn't always work out that way. The least amount of preparation time is 1 week. A teacher cannot expect an art instructor to come up with an integrated lesson overnight. And integration should work both ways. The classroom teacher should also reinforce what is going on in the art room as much as possible.

Technology now plays a very important part in my integration of art into the curriculum. Before I had access to the Internet, I contacted all my adopted artists by mail. I waited for several weeks or months before hearing from some of our adoptees. This is not the case since I've been on-line; I usually hear from the artists within 1 or 2 days. Also, I now make connections myself with foreign schools via the Internet instead of relying on being matched with another school by organizations such as U.S.S.E.A. (U.S. Society for Education through Art). Here again, time is saved because of the immediacy of the process.

When making arrangements for an art exchange with a school in a foreign country, make sure you are able to speak the language. It is difficult working through an interpreter. This is why I only contact schools where English is spoken by someone. I never exchange more than 25 pieces of artwork, and these pieces are never matted or mounted. I try to do everything I can to keep the weight down because of postage. I always make sure the exchanges are permanent so that the pieces won't have to be mailed back to the original address. I also like to include photographs of our school and surrounding area and a recent local newspaper so that the foreign students will be able to learn more about us.

When creating books by using the Illustory kits from Chimeric, make sure you allow plenty of time for the books to be bound and returned from the company. Sometimes this may take several months. For the past 2 years, we have mailed our kits in the spring and have received the completed books during the summer. Because our fourth-grade students transfer to another school at the beginning of the fifth grade, we invite all of them back for a book signing in which the authors and illustrators sign the copies of the books that are to be kept in our school library. Copies of these books may also be ordered individually for a reasonable price. Many of our students (or their parents) order personal copies for themselves and family members.

The Four Steps of Art Criticism

Susan Gabbard
Oklahoma City, Oklahoma

Plato said, "Wonder is the feeling of philosophy, and philosophy begins in wonder." Educators know that one fundamental joy of teaching is to witness and share in the wonder of learning. Wonder seizes and overwhelms us and sparks creativity. Looking at art can transport students to another world as they wonder and investigate their way through a work of art. The educator serves as a kind of mediator between the world of wonder and the wonder of a student. The experience of looking at and exploring a piece of artwork implores students to think. This process of developing critical-thinking skills increases in students when educators encourage philosophical inquiry through dialogue about a work of art.

A quality art program includes the study of art criticism, art history, aesthetics, and art production. Anyone teaching art has the responsibility to teach students to think about art and to realize that art involves the mind as well as the hand. Art production is making and creating works of art. This comes naturally to students in elementary school and provides time for an activity that is also fun and usually relaxing. Many resources are available to teachers on art production.

Art history gives students a sense of time and place. Learning about the history of art is learning about the beginning of time and how human beings have communicated with each other and developed cultures that have long valued both beautiful and functional works of art. These works include architectural structures, woven patterns in fabric, objects of adornment, sculptural icons, as well as drawings, paintings, and prints. Using art objects to teach students about the history of the world enhances the learning tenfold.

Aesthetics is having an appreciation for all that is beautiful. In today's complex society, the ability to recognize and enjoy higher levels of creativity and beauty is extremely important. Developing aesthetic perception gives students the ability to use all the senses at the same time. We live in a highly materialistic and technological culture. Students need the ability to make good decisions about what they do and do not want to look at. Thinking and making decisions is what art is all about. A student or artist faced with a blank sheet of paper or an empty canvas must decide where the first mark will be. How long, how wide, what color, what shape, and how much space are all decisions that must be made at either the conscious or subconscious level of thinking. Little do students realize how much thinking is going on when they are enjoying themselves so much!

Art criticism is the process of studying, understanding, and judging artworks. An *art critic* is a person who practices art criticism as a job or profession. The objectives of the four steps of art criticism are simple and easy to teach to students of any age. The word *criticism* should not scare or intimidate students. They learn that, through art criticism, they will use logical steps as they carefully study and examine works of art for meanings or messages conveyed by the artists in a visual way. The students will gather facts and information similar to the way an attorney or scientist would, to help them form judgments about artworks. Once learned, this process can be applied to the students' own artwork and will help them improve their skills and learn more about making visual statements. Now let's look at the four steps of art criticism.

How to Teach the Four Steps of Art Criticism

Open the lesson with a short discussion of the word *criticism.* Have students ever heard this word? What do they think it means? Explain that criticism does not always mean a negative or something bad. In art, the word is used when a person takes a really good look at something artistic and learns more about it. It is a way to help artists and students make better artworks. Begin by selecting a reproduction of a painting that is in a book or at a local art museum. Even a postcard of a painting can be used.

Step 1: Describe

In this step, students tell only the facts. They should make a list of things they see in the painting. The students should not say anything about what they think the picture is about. Save that thought for Step 3. For example, if the painting is a portrait, they will say, "I see a picture of a person." Students should describe the type of clothing the person is wearing. If they can see the background, they should describe what is there: "I see a room with a window and a desk."

Step 2: Analyze

In Step 2, students will look for the elements and principles of art. The elements are color, line, shape, texture, space, and value. The principles are balance, pattern, emphasis, unity and variety, rhythm, and proportion. Students must have some understanding of each of these so that they can look for them in the painting.

Step 3: Interpretation

This is the step where students can say what they think the painting is about. They may have different opinions about the painting and its meaning, and that's OK. Here, they must tell how the painting makes them feel or how the artist felt when he or she painted it.

Step 4: Evaluate or Judge

The last step gives students the opportunity to decide whether they like the painting and whether they think it is a good work of art. This answer should be an opinion based on all the facts and information the students have gathered.

Remember that once this process is understood and students are familiar with how to do the steps, they can begin to use this exercise on their own artwork. Students can use this tool to evaluate their progress throughout the school year and learn how to improve the work they do in visual art, as well as in the other subjects they study in school.

Readings

Chapman, L. (1992). *Art: Images and ideas.* Worcester, MA: Davis.

Hrebenach, E. (1980). A rationale for aesthetic education. *Art Teacher, 10*(1), 25.

Martin, F. W. (1987). Sir Joshua Reynold's "Invention": Intellectual activity as a foundation of art. *Art Education, 40*(6), 6.

Mittler, G., & Ragans, R. (1992). *Exploring art.* Lake Forest, IL: Glencoe/ Macmillan/McGraw-Hill.

▩ Rhythmic Games

Barry K. Elmore
Chicago, Illinois

One of my favorite activities that works with all elementary grade levels is rhythmic games. It is used to call the class to order and gets the full attention of all students. I clap various rhythms and ask the class to repeat them back to me. This becomes a challenge for them to repeat exactly what I've done. I can make the rhythms more complex by increasing the length and by adding thigh slaps.

With my younger students, I tell them I am going to give them a difficult rhythm, and then I act shocked when they can correctly repeat it. This can be expanded into a music lesson by asking students to identify the meter (e.g., duple, triple, quadruple). You can also select students to clap rhythms the class must repeat.

Weaving Music Through the Curriculum

Fred Koch
Lake Forest, Illinois

Music has the ability to create a very natural connection with an assortment of classroom activities, including science, mathematics, and social studies. At the primary level, though, one of the easiest and most powerful ways to integrate music is through language arts experiences with the use of songs. Children at this age are so innately musical. Singing, dancing, and playing with language is an unconstrained part of their daily experience.

Making music come alive in the classroom is sometimes another story. The main drawback is that many classroom teachers feel inadequate when it comes to bringing music activities to their students. This is not uncommon. I see this everywhere I go. Even the most gifted teachers, many of whom love music themselves and in their hearts know that music is a vital part of the childhood experience, just do not believe that they have the tools necessary to pull it off. Often, they think that they have to be "musicians" themselves or insist that they possess an awful singing voice and couldn't bear to unleash it in front of a class full of students.

So, the first step in getting to the point of feeling comfortable with music is to confront these two common misconceptions. To confront the first misconception, if you value music, you need to find ways of showing it to your students. Students need to be involved in a classroom culture where teachers exhibit attitudes and behaviors that reinforce music as a meaningful part of life.

Confronting the second misconception has to do with your comfort level in singing. For many of us, using songs is probably the easiest and most basic way to integrate music into our classrooms. This doesn't mean you have to strap on a guitar or take a year's worth of piano lessons. This is where recordings can be so useful. The work has been done for you. All you need to do is spend a little preparation time listening to some recordings to find songs that will help support the subject you have in mind. Listen to the song with an ear to whether it will be appealing to the sensibilities of your students.

You will find no lack of available recordings out there in the commercial world. If I relied on the songs found in my music series at school, I would soon run into difficulty. I find many of the songs I use at my public library. Many children's sections now have a growing collection of CDs and cassette tapes.

So, if you truly are uncomfortable with the prospect of singing along with your students, test the waters by singing along with some recordings. Wordsheets, overheads, and sentence strips are all support materials that can detract the focus from you and your singing to the song. You might be surprised how much fun you can have with your students when you are enjoying music together.

Helpful Tips

I have really enjoyed observing fellow teachers as they begin their adventure into music. One of the more obvious and safer methods of bringing music into the classroom is simply to have music playing as your students come in. Most transitional times are good opportunities to feature music. Bring in some of your favorite recordings. You don't have to make a big presentation about it. Have some music playing and see what happens.

Recorded music also works well for quiet times. A little Mozart can be very effective at calming the atmosphere. (Music deserves to be played on the best equipment possible, so do what you can to have a quality sound system in your room.)

Other teachers have experienced success incorporating a regularly scheduled "Musical Show-and-Tell" time. It is a chance for students to make presentations that relate to the music in their own lives. This can be a song they sing for the class, an instrument (authentic or homemade) they bring from home, a book with a musical theme, or a recording they enjoy listening to at home. If a piano is available somewhere, encourage students who take piano lessons to share some music they have learned. Once the stage is set for sharing, even those who don't take lessons will want to play a song they have learned from a friend or relative.

If you have a music teacher in your building, he or she can be a great resource, not only for making recommendations for musical recordings and songs but also for helping reinforce concepts from your classroom curricular materials. More and more curricular materials are including songs and musical examples that correlate with their units. Countless storybooks are also designed to be sung, everything from "There Was an Old Lady Who Swallowed a Fly" to Louis Armstrong's "What a Wonderful World." But if you're not quite ready to take that on yet, find the time to collaborate with the music teacher.

Most music teachers I know are more than happy to support teacher efforts by presenting some of these ideas during their time with your students. In our school district, we have even set aside planning time for the art and music specialists to meet with classroom teachers to develop cooperative lessons. The goal is to create a climate where music is welcomed and celebrated. Before long, music becomes a natural and living part of the classroom. Music becomes a segment of the school experience students really look forward to and enjoy.

CHAPTER **10**

Creative Scheduling

$\mathcal{H}$ere are two examples of daily schedules.

Chapter Overview

- ➡ **Pam Peters**, a kindergarten and first-grade teacher at Rossmoor Elementary School in Los Alamitos, California, presents a full-day kindergarten schedule.

- ➡ **Tarry Lindquist**, fourth- and fifth-grade teacher at Lakeridge Elementary School in Mercer Island, Washington, shares her split class schedule and block period.

A Full-Day Kindergarten Schedule

Pam Peters
Los Alamitos, California

Our kindergarten is considered a full-day program. Here is a brief outline of my daily schedule:

7:45 a.m.	Children arrive, playground or indoor play until 8:00 a.m.
8:00 a.m.	Opening: daily news, flag, "Math Their Way" calendar work, planning for the day, roll, and lunch count
8:20 a.m.	Thematic activities: shared reading, songs, pocket chart activities, interactive writing, literature and discussion
9:00 a.m.	Writing/PE: We have an instructional assistant who works with each classroom for 30 minutes daily. We use her for a PE pullout program, so we can work inside with half the class. While she is with one group, I do modeled writing and journal writing with the other group. (Teachers plan the PE program, and she implements our plans.)
9:30 a.m.	Mathematics: Whole-group lesson, then individual, paired, or cooperative group activities
10:15 a.m.	Recess
10:30 a.m.	Guided reading groups: Parent volunteers work in the classroom during this time. I work with two or three groups a day. During a group, we learn heavy-duty work, manipulate magnetic letters to spell the word several times, do some guided writing using the day's word, and then reread a known text and learn a new text. Parents supervise other activities: science investigations, computer games, Bingo, reading in the room, buddy reading, and art.
11:20 a.m.	Lunch
12:00 p.m.	A variety of things go on during the afternoon: singing, movement, literature, dramatic play, science, social science, blocks, puppetry, choice time, art.
1:15 p.m.	Cleanup and dismiss
1:15–2:15 p.m.	Prep time

Helpful Tips

I believe that a kindergarten classroom should be flexible and reflect the children's interests and experiences. I am never too strict about following my plans if something comes up that needs attention. The frustration I feel about not ever getting to everything is great! I have begun to alternate days on some activities. For example, I would love to do interactive writing daily, but I find it better to alternate with dramatizations of stories. At least that way, the children are getting a wide variety of opportunities.

A Split-Grade Class Schedule

Tarry Lindquist
Mercer Island, Washington

My classroom is a self-contained four/five split. Half of my 26 students are fourth graders, and half are fifth graders. My fourth graders become my next year's fifth graders, as I keep half my class each year. After nearly 20 years of teaching fifth graders only, I find this split class exciting and educationally valuable for my students and for me.

Fifty percent of my students know each other, me, and the classroom routine that second year. They are ready to take on leadership roles, guiding and mentoring the new fourth graders and helping me as soon as school starts. From the very first day of the new year, it is obvious that the classroom is "ours," not just mine. Such immediate student ownership changes the dynamics of our relationship all year in a way that I think is more positive and more democratic.

As for me, I get to live with the results of last year's teaching, and believe me, I have learned a lot. The best part is observing students in September performing skills and behaving in ways they couldn't in June. I find that my teaching is shaped by the holes I find as well. I am challenged to explore other ways to teach a previously introduced skill. I am pushed to provide additional, often innovative, appropriate practice because of that dreaded worst phrase in the intermediate grades—"We've done that!" Finally, I have the opportunity to re-do (or un-do!) what is misunderstood, mistaken, or just plain forgotten.

Disclaimer: This is my perfect schedule. It happens 1 day a week, maybe. The rest of the time, specialists' slots dance across my day, students are pulled out for one reason or another, assemblies zip in and out, and I am left wondering where half of my class is.

9:15–9:20 a.m.	Opening
9:20–9:50 a.m.	Specialist (PE, music, or library)
9:50–10:55 a.m.	Mathematics
10:55–11:10 a.m.	Recess
11:30 a.m.– 12:50 p.m.	Block Note: I work very hard to protect this one period because it is the linchpin of each day (see description below).
12:50–1:30 p.m.	Lunch and recess
1:30–2:30 p.m.	Reader's workshop
2:30–2:45 p.m.	Recess
2:45–3:30 p.m.	Spelling or computer lab

Block

About 15 years ago, I was concerned about the lack of cohesiveness during the day for my students and for me. I began experimenting by integrating content, skills, and attitudes across the curriculum. The first connection I made was between reading and social studies. Using our reading series of that time, I found stories that connected in some way with social studies topics.

It didn't take long to leave the basal text behind and to begin collecting chapter books that introduced, enhanced, or extended social studies or science topics. I found, before long, that themes did bring the day together, providing a wholeness that had been missing. For me, most of the themes came from social studies topics or concepts.

Soon, I was wrapping 90% of my day around a single social studies theme. What we read and wrote about tied into the theme. Our art extended our understanding and appreciation of the theme. The "block" was born. Rather than have a separate language arts period, art period, social studies period, and science period, we now have block.

Block is often an integration of two or more disciplines. The block period provides time for extended study, depth, and integrated projects revealing student engagement and understanding. For example, block may begin with a discussion about what the world was like in late 1400s and early 1500s. After completing an informal KWL (What We Know, What We Want to Know, What We Learned) Chart, I might read aloud from *1492*, a picture book about different European and Asian cities in that time.

Then I might introduce the students to different explorers and ask them to choose one to research. Each student would research in both print and computer resources, completing a data disk (see my book *Seeing the Whole Through Social Studies,* 1995) of basic information. A mini lesson reviewing research skills provides the fundamentals for additional language arts practice.

As students finish the disks, they are encouraged to use the Internet to find examples of kinds of clothing their explorers might have worn, what kinds of foods they might have eaten, what sorts of ships they might have sailed in, and so on to share the next day. And that's just the first day of the social studies unit "Contact: Europeans Come to a New World," which explores the history of contact, as well as the relationships between native peoples and Europeans in the Americas.

The same day in reader's workshop, students are reading *Morning Girl,* Michael Dorris's book about the Taino people, the people Columbus met when he first came ashore more than 500 years ago. Additionally, I read from picture books such as Jane Yolen's *Encounter* and Michael Foreman's *The Boy Who Sailed With Columbus.* That's our first day. By the end of the unit, the students have created mini personal billboards of the explorers in period dress (see billboards in my book *Seeing the Whole Through Social Studies*). Wearing the billboards, the students present their explorers through first-person biography speeches.

This year, my students decided that the explorers were like mechanical toys, so they cut coin slots in each of their billboards and then created tokens from tag board. Arranging to use the school library, they invited five second-grade classes to come to their Mini Explorer's Mechanical Museum. Each visitor was given five tokens. By putting a token in the slot in a personal billboard, the speaker "came to life" and gave a 1-minute introduction to the explorer and then became inanimate again. As we assessed the event afterward, my students found that they gave their speeches an average of 18 times in 1 hour! (Nothing like a mathematics connection, too.)

Helpful Tips

Connect as much as possible throughout the day to give students a sense of wholeness of what they are studying. Important things, like ideas, concepts, attitudes, and skills, do not fit into little artificial boxes you only take out for 50 minutes three times a week or for 20 minutes a day. Move away from fragmenting learning by disciplines to integrating across the curriculum, and you will see your students become more engaged, more enthusiastic, and more successful. Plus, it's more fun!

CHAPTER **11**

Experiencing Education Abroad

*I*magine traveling to Chinan, Korea, to meet key pals or visiting an elementary school in Hanamaki, Japan.

Chapter Overview

- **Margaret Holtschlag**, a fourth-grade teacher at Murphy Elementary School in Haslett, Michigan, discusses what began as a key pal project and turned into real friendship between children and communities half a world away.

- **Robert Harper**, an elementary music teacher at William Floyd Elementary School in Shirley, New York, explains what America can learn from Japanese education. He says that both nations can learn from each other and that it is in their mutual best interests to share what they know in guiding future world leaders.

173

▧ Haslett, Michigan-Chinan, Korea Partnership

Margaret Holtschlag
Haslett, Michigan

In my 20 years of teaching, I could not have predicted I would be in an airplane with 14 children on our way to visit friends in Korea for spring break. But what began as a key pal project turned into real friendship between children and between communities half a world away. It has been a most amazing journey—traveling through cyberspace and across continents and oceans—to pursue friendship with the people of Chinan, Korea.

The Chinan, Korea-Haslett, Michigan partnership began in March 1996, when I was asked whether I would like to have my students write to children in rural Korea. We were being asked to pilot a program for Global Youth Network, a national endeavor in Korea to connect their rural areas with the outside world. My students had previously been engaged in a complex study of cross-cultural issues, beginning with a study of their own personal histories and then research about the United Nations, so they responded enthusiastically to this request. To my students, this was just another way of making new friends, but their correspondence has become a model for the creation of other partnerships between teachers in Korea and Michigan.

The children began writing once or twice a week, first with polite questions that quickly blossomed into lively, fun letters in which the children talked about their lives in Korea and Michigan. Sending e-mail meant lots of letters could be sent and quick responses could be received. Each time we sent a package, it took 10 days and several dollars to mail, but with technology we could write as often as we wanted. Ms. Mija Moon (the Korean students' teacher) and I also wrote about our schools and our personal lives and became friends too. Each group had a natural curiosity to learn about each other's countries, and my students began paying attention to the news when Korea was in the headlines. Mija and I planned weekly topics for the children to write about, such as family structure, holidays, the meanings of their names, responsibilities at home, favorite subjects in school, the view from the school, and goals for their futures. Ms. Ae-Jin Kang, a graduate student at Michigan State University, visited our class to teach weekly lessons about Korea's history, culture, and language.

The classroom project soon expanded to the community when Ms. Moon brought several children and parents to Michigan to visit in August 1996. Murphy Elementary School families hosted this 10-day visit with home stays and activities for the children to learn more about each other's cultures. The children played basketball, went for a hayride, danced the Macarena, and went to a Lansing Lugnuts baseball game, all the while learning about America.

The people of Chinan, Korea, then invited us to visit them, and I took 14 children, mostly fourth and fifth graders, and several parents to Korea for 10 days in April 1997. Part of our trip was sponsored by the *Chosun Daily,* the national newspaper in Korea. We saw a beautiful country with friendly, generous people. When our bus pulled into Chinan, a tiny town at the foot of Mai Mountain, we felt that we were "home," after all the letters between the children. The people of Chinan showed us their schools, homes, mountains, and the beauty of their country. Although language was a struggle, we sang together and laughed often. The children sang "Muh-reeh, Uh-kkae, Mooh-rup, Bal" ("Heads, Shoulders, Knees, Toes") and "Arriang," a traditional Korean song, as well as "Michigan, My Michigan."

On the last night before returning home, Korean and American parents joined in a circle and sang a love song that surpassed any language and any distance. We learned so much about Korea because of their friendship and generosity. From the beginning, we were only a keystroke away from talking with our friends. Although the children have all moved on to middle school, many of them continue to correspond. Parents in Chinan and Haslett continue to write. And Mija and I have continued the project as we introduced our third group of children to each other this February.

Information about this project has been reported in the *Lansing State Journal, Towne Courier,* and *Chosun Daily.* The project has been highlighted in an Internet training series produced by Ingham County Integrated School District. In November 1996, the Korean Broadcasting System filmed the children in Haslett and in Chinan as part of a documentary about innovative uses of technology to help children learn about the world. This program was aired throughout Korea in February 1997.

I have spoken at education conferences about the Global Youth Network project and its benefits to enhancing the writing curriculum and encompassing a personal and global view of the world. I have also talked about the management tricks to make it possible. Here are a few of those suggestions.

Get personal with the teacher of the children with whom you are corresponding. Form a personal connection and find commonalities beyond the classroom. This can be done with frequent e-mails and with a telephone call or two. A strong friendship between the teachers can carry the project through the more hectic times in the school year when the letters tend to be less frequent.

Invite people in the community to speak to your class about the country or state of your key pals. This firsthand narrative can give a real-life connection to your students and make the place real to them. It also gets the community involved and can open the door to greater community involvement.

Arrange for common topics to be discussed in e-mail even if it is a loose structure. Otherwise, children can tend to rehash the same topics (e.g., what's your favorite _____). Send photographs, videotapes, artwork, and handwritten notes once in a while; it reinforces the connection with something colorful and tangible that otherwise would only be a black-and-white e-mail. We also sent a box of "Michigan artifacts" to Korea. It was filled with Michigan State University pins and banners, postcards showing Michigan landmarks, sand from Lake Lansing, a Petoskey stone (state stone), tourism brochures, and our daily newspaper.

Parent volunteers can help with the typing in the beginning of the project. Even if your students know keyboarding, having a volunteer help with the typing can accelerate the correspondence when the students' motivation is high. This is a great way to set up a strong foundation. Then, after your students are successful with sending e-mail and getting responses, they can take over with typing their own letters.

Students do not always need to be paired up one-on-one in a key pal project. It's OK to send letters addressed to "Dear Key Pal" and to let several students read the letters. Experiment with the most effective (and most frequent) procedure that fits your students.

Call the local newspaper office and tell the editor about the project. The public wants to hear good news about the schools! It is also a great way to initiate networking among educators who read about your project and want to learn more.

Let the project evolve. The students will direct the way on the basis of the letters they write. If they own the project, they will soon expand their writing in complex ways.

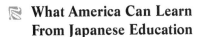 What America Can Learn From Japanese Education

Robert Harper
Shirley, New York

If it is true that education is the security of a nation, then this great country must find current global comparisons of scholasticism rather unsettling. The recent Third International Math and Science Studies (TIMSS) Report focused attention on junior high school achievement in those two disciplines. The results ranked the United States 28th out of 41 nations in mathematics and 17th in science, whereas Japan, for example, ranked as one of the top three nations. What is it about Japan's educational philosophies and practices that dramatically distances its students' achievements from ours? The American myth of a high student suicide rate being the high price of such excellence is more sour grapes than fact. The tragic truth is that U.S. students have the statistical edge over their Japanese counterparts in this area.

One of the most significant differences between the two countries is curriculum. Whereas Americans pride themselves on state and local control of what is to be studied when, Japanese have a central Ministry of Education, Science, Sports and Culture, known as *Monbusho,* that promotes a national curriculum. Monbusho contends that education provides a sound base for a nation's development and that, to this end, the government must guide its youngest citizens in their growth as people who have "rich hearts as well as healthy minds and bodies." This sound base is provided by fewer topics covered annually than in an equivalent American curriculum, but these topics are covered in greater depth, requiring less review in later grades. For example, in Japan, first-grade mathematics thoroughly covers 7 topics, but in the United States, *Addison-Wesley Mathematics* challenges American first-grade teachers to cover 25 topics.

The structure of the Japanese school year is also conducive to mastery learning. With 220 student days, there are fewer gaps in the school year for students to forget material or to regress in skills; thus, less review is needed on the students' return from a vacation. Even when school is not in session, learning continues, as it is not unusual for assignments to be given in these interim times. Even though Japanese teachers spend long hours at school, only about 4 hours per day are spent actually teaching, the rest being filled with collegial collaboration, lesson preparation, or grading student work.

In one elementary school I visited in Hanamaki, the student day, though 8 hours long, had its academic sessions punctuated by a vigorous 5- to 10-minute recess every hour. I observed greater student attentiveness (hence, greater learning) resulting from these scheduled breaks from learning. Nor is the instruction time between the breaks devoted to intense chunking of language, mathematics, science, and social studies, for one third of the Japanese elementary day is nonacademic.

As Monbusho's goal is to promote the well-rounded development of the nation, it provides a comprehensive and integrated educational experience for all learners that includes music, drawing and handicrafts, homemaking, physical education, special activities (culturally related), and moral education. This last discipline is rather foreign to the American education system as it is the explicit and mandated teaching of societal values. Every day, Japan prepares its youngest citizens for personally fulfilling and responsible adulthood by infusing into daily lessons its standards, such as cooperation and teamwork, integrity, respect for nature, honesty, appreciation of beauty, and promising to honor the public good.

For its efforts, Japan is rewarded with, among other advantages, one of the lowest crime rates in the world. This distinction impressed me in a personal way when I had to leave Tokyo for another prefecture without my luggage, which was to be picked up later and forwarded. I was directed to just leave my suitcase on the sidewalk to await transit. When I began to protest that it was unwise to just leave my suitcase on the sidewalk in front of a major Tokyo hotel in anticipation of its being transported by individuals I did not know, my apprehensions were not even understood. Of course, I was reunited with my luggage as my Japanese hosts had fully expected.

Just as a Kyoto pine tree cannot be expected to survive transplantation to the sand of Arizona or the rocky coast of Maine, the ideology and methodology of Japan cannot be directly imported and applied to U.S. schools. Although the educational missions are the same—to prepare children to work cooperatively and undistracted by the irrationality of bias—the particulars of what and how to teach need to be adapted. Still, both nations can learn much from each other, and it is in their mutual best interests to share what they know in guiding future world leaders.

(Note: Education professionals interested in experiencing the Japanese education system should contact the Fulbright Memorial Fund, 1400 K Street, NW, Suite 650, Washington, DC 20005-2403.)

CHAPTER **12**

Topic Smorgasbord

Sharing More Key Elementary Issues and Perspectives

*H*ere are more key elementary issues and perspectives. These topics do not fit neatly into any of the previous chapters but are valuable tips for teachers.

Chapter Overview

- **Catherine B. Harper**, a second-grade teacher at Tangier Smith Elementary School in Mastic Beach, New Jersey, shares her Class Creed, a statement of ethos and intellectual and aesthetic intent.

- **Suzy Ables**, a kindergarten teacher at Huber Ridge Elementary School in Westerville, Ohio, describes her kindergarten classroom.

- **Carol B. Avila**, a first-grade teacher at Main Street School in Warren, Rhode Island, goes beyond books. Her first-grade students can find "*f* of *x*" in algebra by using a "Beat the Algebra Machine," which she made.

- **Katherine C. Falso**, a middle childhood generalist, says that no course, degree, workshop, institute, certification, or honor could equal the substance and endurance of having good colleagues.

- **Brenda Hartshorn**, a multiage primary-grade teacher at Moretown Elementary School in Moretown, Vermont, discusses the changing role of a paraeducator from the perspective of a classroom teacher.

- **Mark Wagler**, a fourth- and fifth-grade teacher at Randall Elementary School in Madison, Wisconsin, is part of an informal teacher network. Wagler says that together the staff write grants, develop projects, share curriculum ideas uncommon in their buildings, cultivate community partnerships, produce conferences and publications, and more.

- **David V. Buus**, a second-grade teacher at Moorcroft Elementary School in Moorcroft, Wyoming, surprises his students at the beginning of the year with a new theme.

- **Maggie Lee Costa**, a career education coordinator at the Stanislaus County Office of Education in Modesto, California, has the students evaluate her at the end of the school year.

- **Arlene Arp**, a kindergarten teacher at Avondale Elementary School in Avondale Estates, Georgia, describes academic center time.

- **Fran Goldenberg**, a fourth-grade teacher at William H. Ray Elementary School in Chicago, Illinois, says that teachers at her school don't play politics.

The Class Creed

Catherine B. Harper
Mastic Beach, New Jersey

Filling in for me when I took a professional leave day, the substitute teacher for my class paid me a gratifying compliment. She took a copy of my Class Creed, which I had included in my lesson plans, and shared it with teachers in the other buildings where she substitutes. Today, my Class Creed is celebrated by my second-grade New Yorkers, as well as by at least one high school class in Alaska and who knows how many classes in between as it has been circulated among educators all over the country.

What is this creed? It is a 237-word statement of ethos, of intellectual and aesthetic intent. My second graders dramatically recite it from memory and heart every morning, complete with body gestures accompanying every phrase, as we remind ourselves each day of our purpose.

In a time when the basic family structure is changing in its ability to support, nurture, and ready the child to succeed in school and in life, teachers must center their efforts on building a community of learners who value developing their character. The Class Creed, which I compiled from sundry sage sources, empowers my children with a moral compass, unites us in our efforts to learn, and promotes self-direction and self-correction. For example, when children transgress a class or building rule, as a disciplinary action I use a relevant element from the creed as a basis for the children's understanding of what they have done and what they must do to restore a relationship or situation. The creed offers a touchstone for encouragement, a validation for being respectful, responsible, and resourceful.

Beginning on the first day of school, I use visualization techniques to assist the children in memorizing a new line each day. It takes until mid-October for them to learn to say the creed well. It takes until the end of the year for them to learn to live the creed well.

The Class Creed

I am a self-reliant and reliable individual. I believe that society does not owe me anything. I will not be paid for having a brain, but rather for using my brain.

I will be a lifter, not a leaner; a learner, not a loser. I will give myself to learning and develop my thinking, civilize my heart, and give wings to my imagination. I will grow to appreciate the beauty of Art and Music. I will become best friends to Truth, Honor, and Respect.

Discouragement will never defeat me because I know that I can move a mountain by first carrying away the small stones and then continuing patiently.

I am responsible for myself. I make my own choices and accept the consequences. I cannot blame television nor my friends, parents, or teachers for my mistakes. Failure is not the enemy of success. I must pull apart my mistakes, looking for the reason where I went wrong, and then use my mistakes, not for stumbling blocks, but for stepping stones.

I will, especially when nobody is looking, do all the good I can to all the people I can in all the ways I can as often as I can for as long as I can. The happiness I give away will turn again to shine on me, and I will let others light their own candles on the warmth and radiance of my service and success.

Kindergarten Ideas

Suzy Ables
Westerville, Ohio

In our classroom, activities are hands-on, so children have the opportunity to use all three learning channels simultaneously and to experience as much success as possible. There is continuous observation and assessment, diagnosis, and then teaching of the particular skills needed. Each teacher-directed lesson is tailored to include a broad range of skills; questions and tasks go to children according to experiences needed by each child. Small-group instruction is based on common needs. The most time, however, is spent individually in journaling, shared reading, or skills practice between either child and teacher, child and volunteer, child and her or his reading partner, or child and her or his cooperative learning partner.

To make learning meaningful, I consistently and continuously provide activities that use kindergarten skills in a real way. Each week, we have a cooking activity. We first, as a class, write the recipe; this necessitates the children having to list the needed steps sequentially and to help me spell the words. Next, the children help make the "grocery list." The following day, small groups come to the cooking table to read back and follow the step-by-step recipe and to eat their concoctions. All recipes are designed to make individual portions so that each child can do 100% of the cooking and also be able to reproduce the food at home with minimal adult help.

Each week, we also produce class books that are extensions of shared literature. These are all easily read by kindergartners because the text is predictable, follows a pattern, and has minimal change from page to page. We regularly ensure the quality of the needed picture clues by taking class photographs for the illustrations, providing both recognizable illustrations as well as extremely high motivation to reread the book.

The midyear activity that focuses on the need for mathematics skills and working together is our class Valentine candy sale. We take orders for the candy, graph our ordering progress daily, tally the amount of candy needed to fill our orders, order our supplies, make the candy (complete with science lessons involving germ cultures), fill the individual boxes (usually just over 500!), and fill each order (about 75). Once we have determined our profit, we graph our color preference for T-shirts; then, we each contribute a drawing and a signature for the silk screen design before taking a trip to the local T-shirt shop where we use our profit to buy and silk-screen our own class T-shirts.

This year, after the children and I wrote our classroom mission statement, I realized that the children had come up with a list of my beliefs about education. (Keep in mind that these are "at-risk" $5\frac{1}{2}$-year-old children.) As they listed the reasons why we were in school, their child language paralleled the basics of mental, social, emotional, and physical development; they already realized that working exclusively on one of these facets without the others would result in unhappy children who were not at all well-rounded children.

The children knew that most planning and preparation should be my responsibility, as would be the physical logistics of caring for them as we combined children from four schools and 16 classrooms. They also realized quite quickly that some responsibility rested on them if education were to take place: "You can't do things that might hurt people or our stuff, that might make people unhappy, or that might keep people from learning." If you think about it, this really covers everything! At this point, my philosophy dictated that I had to help the children develop the interpersonal skills necessary to carry out this philosophy. I believe in the use of words to solve problems, especially the word *because*. (In our classroom, you must tell someone "why.")

The fact that I am a very consistent person allows me regularly to turn problems back to the children so that they may learn how to solve the problems (with my support and encouragement) and feel confident and successful. Consistency allows the environment to remain equally safe and secure for the children no matter how divergent our days may be.

Beyond Books

Carol B. Avila
Warren, Rhode Island

I like the challenge of teaching to high national standards. The standards require that I teach for meaning and make the lessons relevant. What is taught in school should be connected to life outside the classroom, so I go beyond the books.

Here is a 6-year-old's civics lesson: Once, my first grade class petitioned the Warren Town Council to plant bulbs in front of the town hall (we had won a grant of 250 flowering bulbs). The children used invented spelling in the letter to the council, in their thank-you notes, and in their blueprints for the Warren Planning Board. They practiced their new measuring skills to design the blueprints. They read many letters and notes and newspaper articles about themselves.

Each year, we end our Newtonian physics studies about motion, gravity, and force by entering a children-built "contraption" in the Warren Preservation Society's Warren On Wheels parade. The children get to mess around with some great hands-on science and support a local organization. For the past 2 years, my class has received first prize in this People's Choice competition.

My children can find "f of x" in algebra. Yes, the same thing that successfully turned me off mathematics can be done by 6-year-olds. I just didn't like, nor could my children understand, an abstract "function machine" graphic in the mathematics textbook. So, I went to the high school folks and learned the basis of what I was supposed to be teaching the children. I then made a big silver "Beat the Algebra" Machine. It has a slot for the "input" number and slot for the "output." A child sits inside and adds (or subtracts) the same amount to each number that comes into the machine. The children look for a pattern. This is algebraic thinking and is highly recommended by the National Council of

Teachers of Mathematics. It is a bit watered down, limiting the function to "subtracting" instead of adding by a negative, but give my children the input and output data and they will think algebraically and tell you what is happening in the algebra machine!

We work with the Warren Land Conservation Trust. Each year, we begin our literacy skills by reading and writing about our beautiful sea-shore. Our studies are based on the NRC's Standards for Elementary Life Sciences. We visit the wetlands and do the same water quality test-ing done by conservationists. We take a shoreline survey of organisms—including people—and record the data. We create a classroom atlas of the beach full of my little ones' first attempts at using the alphabetic principle. They love to read and write about our bay, and the Land Trust is delighted to teach them conservation while they are young.

We learn the concept "word" by pointing to words we are singing. The children have songs we sing in their three-ring binders. They prac-tice speech-to-print matching—a fundamental of literacy acquisition—while singing. It is a great way to learn this concept because they already know the words to the songs. The best songs are the rousing patriotic types, and I like the children to have mastered the skill by Veterans Day. We join the veterans at their ceremony on November 11, and the chil-dren's beautiful singing brings tears to everyone's eyes. They are very appreciative. The children also research the veterans in their families and write about these relatives. The stories are hung on a "Wall of Thanks" during the ceremony.

We study the base 10 principle while conducting penny drives. This year, we collected pennies for leukemia, and a year ago one of our fami-lies lost their home and possessions in a fire; that year, the pennies went to help them. The children practice their skip counting and grouping while making piles of 10 pennies and then cups of 100.

In Grade 1, I don't have enough time to do anything except teach reading, writing, and arithmetic. But in the 21st century, there will be no time to waste on anybody who cannot think for her- or himself and who is not actively making the community a better place in which to live. So, I teach the basics as part of a year-long course in good citi-zenship and thinking. Every one of the national standards recommends this.

Helpful Tips

- Give young children "job schedules" so that you can get to the small-group and one-on-one instruction that effectively addresses literacy instruction for beginner readers and writers.

- Know the national standards and keep learning as much as you can from them.

- Know that school is training for the real world, so get the local paper, know the community, and direct instruction toward something truly meaningful to the students.

▨ Learning With and From Our Colleagues

Katherine C. Falso
Melrose Park, Pennsylvania

I have been thinking about the similarities between birding and teaching. A naturalist once told me that most people never look much above the horizon as they go about their lives. They miss a great many birds that way. Birding really begins with the discipline of looking up. Age, however, is giving me a natural decline. I find myself frequently searching the ground, gathering my thoughts, and looking for insights. I have to remind myself to change my point of view.

It is the same with teaching. In student-centered classrooms, successful teaching is synonymous with successful students. It is assumed that the source of this success lies in the teacher and her or his lesson plans, materials, and pedagogy. I would like to take a moment to refocus our attention on another overlooked source of our success—our colleagues.

No course, degree, workshop, institute, certification, or honor could equal the substance and endurance of having good colleagues. I have thought about the things I enjoy and need from my fellow teachers and find the following five broad categories.

Renewal

Despite all the wonderful, inspirational books written about all the trials and tribulations of teaching, there is no one I would rather listen to than a colleague who knows me and tells me I have done a good job. When politics and the daily grind wear me down, I know where to find a good shoulder. Colleagues are good listeners. They remember to take me outside, where the trees are big and problems become small. Colleagues always have a good idea or book or lesson to share. They laugh and help me laugh. They are the only ones who get the joke anyway.

Review

Good teachers need good criticism. When trying out new ideas or when the lesson doesn't go as well as planned, I appreciate the colleague who can praise, polish, and question effectively. I need an objective observer of my work.

Confirmation

At times, each of us stands alone, becomes the maverick. Colleagues know how to support each other. Colleagues are knowledgeable about their profession and know exactly what makes a good teacher. They remember to tell me when I do something right.

Refocus

When the lesson doesn't go well, when students' needs become overwhelming, when I've gone on a tangent, my colleagues rein me in. They allow no self-pity; everyone has the same problems. Colleagues help me find positive solutions to discouraging days.

Reunification

Sometimes I feel like a small frog in a small pond. I need a larger picture. That's when I look to my colleagues in other districts, in other states. Teaching needs an occasional infusion of ideas from "outside."

It is stimulating to collect the new ideas and insights of others in our profession. It is also reassuring to learn that others fight the same battles.

When I walk into my classroom, I bring with me not only that dynamic lesson plan but also the wisdom and support of many outstanding teachers. Teaching is an art that we are constantly perfecting. Colleagues understand this and know that we are all on the continuum, not at the goal. Each of our individual successes comes from our collective effort to help each other learn our profession. Here are some things I notice my outstanding colleagues doing:

- Whenever they walk into another classroom, they always hand the teacher a compliment, even before they say what they came to say.

- They smile and call other teachers by name.

- They give fellow teachers credit when using their ideas.

- They freely share ideas because they know that when their ideas get passed around and finally come back, they will be changed and twice as good.

- They point out the "little" things that people do to make their room special.

- They search for positive ways to sort through administrative tangles.

- They share resources, lessons, materials, and time.

- They validate colleagues' ideas by restating them at faculty meetings.

- They support and encourage wise risk taking.

- They make it a point to search out and get to know teachers they don't usually see in a regular day.

- They see a colleague as a whole person, not just someone they know from 8:30 a.m. to 3:30 p.m.

- They eat together. They celebrate birthdays, have faculty breakfasts, go out to dinner once a month, order lunch in, use in-service days to go out to lunch, have picnics. They nosh, diet, dine, and snack together.

The Changing Role of Paraeducators

Brenda Hartshorn
Moretown, Vermont

Elementary education has changed dramatically in the last decade. The more we have learned about child development, learning styles, and learning differences, the more individualized education has become in our schools. A classroom teacher has more needs to meet each day as our profession learns more about the needs of our society and ways we can help children become lifelong learners and ready for the 21st century. Along with changing roles for classroom educators, we have added new jobs to our schools, which have required new job descriptions.

One position added to most elementary classrooms across the country is that of teacher's aide, also known as teaching assistant, paraeducator, and many other similar labels. It seems that we just have not found the title that fits perfectly for these dedicated, talented professionals. For some schools, a teacher's aide may not be a relatively new position over the past few years, but I guarantee you that the job description has changed dramatically for these professionals. A teacher's aide was once a pair of helping hands at mathematics time or reading time in a classroom where you might find a large number of students or many students with high academic needs.

The teacher's aide followed the classroom teacher's directions or plans with a small group of children or worked under a special educator with individuals experiencing learning difficulties. Plans and materials were written and prepared for the aide to follow and use during her or his scheduled hours in the classroom or tutoring space outside the classroom. Minimum wage was the financial compensation for such a job with few if any benefits, such as a small number of allotted sick days. A teacher's aide was often hired at the beginning of or during the school year after a classroom teacher assessed the number and needs of students in her or his classroom. A request to the school board and discussion determined whether there was a need for a position before interviewing and hiring took place.

Currently, because of our knowledge of learning differences, commitment to authentic learning and assessment, individualized instruction, multiage classrooms, Act 230 Inclusion Law, and many other educational practices, teaching assistants are vitally necessary professional staff members. To continue to provide appropriate education to each child with the information about learning that we have gained, we must have the personnel to reach these goals and make it happen. Not only do we depend on each classroom to have at least a part-time aide, but we have hired more talented, experienced people to take the roles of paraeducators.

The term *paraeducator* does not fully identify all these people are and do for our schoolchildren. They are more than a para, or part, of a teacher. They are additional teachers providing quality instruction and care to children. They work side-by-side with classroom teachers, preparing, planning, and implementing instruction and educational experiences for children. Job descriptions for teaching assistants have changed to include most of the same responsibilities as a classroom teacher. Competition for such jobs has become stiffer, with more and more certified and certifiable teachers applying and receiving paraeducator positions.

The hourly wage and benefits have not continued to grow with the job expectations and responsibilities. Getting a pay raise is even tougher for this position than it is for classroom teachers, partly because many people do not know what a paraeducator does for our children during a school day. As one community member said to a paraeducator, "Well, at least it's a job." To a paraeducator, it is more than just a job. Each school day brings new challenges and demands as a paraeducator provides support to classroom teachers and students with a mere 30-minute lunch break. It is a job of giving and interacting with children and adults all day. Most paraeducators will tell you it is an exhausting job but one of great satisfaction from the progress they see children make as they provide support socially, emotionally, and academically.

The Moretown School Board of Directors knows the importance and value of paraeducators in our school. They continue to provide exceptionally qualified people for these jobs each year. The paraeducators we are so fortunate to have give their personal time outside the regular school day. They attend evening meetings and school functions on weekends because they enjoy being a part of children's lives and are unselfishly dedicated to the children's growth and development as citizens and learners. Our paraeducators volunteer to attend team meetings to help work out problems with children. They must keep all they know and hear confidential, which sometimes is difficult as community members may put them in a tough place.

Each of our paraeducators attends workshops and training throughout the school year and summer to increase talents working with children with emotional and academic needs. Two paraeducators recently spent a weekend with two classroom teachers, attending a reading conference so as to better support children involved in a new reading program. Another paraeducator spent several afternoons after school working with a teacher, learning a new way to approach mathematics problem solving within the classroom with young children so that she could extend what the teacher was implementing.

Without our paraeducators, we could not provide the individualized attention and special projects that we are engaged with each day. Our teachers prefer to have them take over as substitute teachers when the regular teachers must be away. The children feel more comfortable with the paraeducator because she or he knows the routines, the expectations, and the children. After all, the paraeducator has been a team member in planning and implementing the educational program.

A paraeducator at Moretown School is more than an extra pair of hands to help tie shoes, zip coats, or supervise playground activity. A new term is needed for this professional position. *Instructional deity* is much closer to the job description than *paraeducator* or *aide*.

Teacher Networks

Mark Wagler
Madison, Wisconsin

Authentic inquiry, community, and communication were several key ideas I wanted to put into practice when I returned to classroom teaching in 1987. I wanted my students to ask and answer their own questions, research their local cultural and natural communities, and present what they learned to larger audiences. Even though Madison schools were the best I had encountered in a decade of freelance storytelling, they still provided inadequate support for what I wanted to accomplish. Staff development, curricular materials, school schedules, evaluation structures, even classroom furniture were all designed for another paradigm.

Today, I am part of an informal teacher network that supports what I most value in teaching. The Heron Network includes about 20 teachers and their classes (Grades 1-6) in 10 Madison-area schools, a few student teachers and graduate students, and some community partners. We keep in regular touch via meetings and several listservs, maintain a Web site, gather three times per year for student conferences, produce a fund-raising variety show, help create museum exhibits, collaborate on a garden project, and gather each June for 2 weeks of research and curriculum development at the Heron Institute.

Our biggest collaborative project is producing the journal *Great Blue: A Journal of Student Inquiry*. Most of our students publish an article or artwork in one of the journal sections: "I Wonder" (science), "Kid-to-Kid" (cultural studies), "Critics & Fanatics" (reading and media literacy), "It Figures!" (mathematics), and "The Gallery" (the arts). Hard copies of the journal become the major texts in our classrooms.

All my classroom instruction (concepts, themes, projects, skill development, homework, field trips, evaluation) is nurtured by the Heron Network. At the Heron Institute, for example, teachers conduct research on daphnia; in my classroom, students collect data from jars of these small lake critters. On our "I Wonder" listserv and in the projects section of our Web site, students discuss daphnia projects. An expert from the University of Wisconsin comes to our classrooms to explore issues of daphnia research. Students present the results of their research on daphnia as displays at our annual Yahara Watershed Fair or as articles in *Great Blue*. Multiply this instance to include family culture, Newberry Award books, algebra, imaginative writing, and scores of other topics to get a big picture of Heron classroom practice.

Not every project includes all Heron classrooms. This year, for example, three of our classrooms are cocreators of "Timewarp," an exhibit at the Madison Children's Museum celebrating Wisconsin's Sesquicentennial. Together, we have researched and imagined how to represent an 1848 pioneer cabin, an 1898 one-room schoolhouse, and a 1948 child's bedroom. With the help of professional videographers, each class is making three or four brief videos documenting 1998 contemporary culture. With the support of a local Internet access provider, each class is helping create a Web site presenting some of our futuristic images for the year 2048.

Our students come from three quite different schools and cultural contexts: (a) a professional neighborhood near the university, (b) a low-income neighborhood with a large percentage of minority students, and (c) a suburban community. These diverse students have shared many ideas via a listserv, taken a joint field trip, examined copies of the same

historical photographs, and soon will meet again at a reception for creators of the "Timewarp" exhibit.

Community partners have been crucial to our success. Besides the
Children's Museum, we work closely with, among others, various pro-
grams and professors at the University of Wisconsin and Edgewood
College, curriculum consultants at the Wisconsin Department of Public
Instruction and in our local districts, and several nature sites. Our most
important partners, though, are our parents.

Because many of our classrooms are multiage, we can establish
multiyear relationships with parents. They come into the classroom to
help with individual student inquiries, field trips and special events, and
typing. Most important, they help their own children plan and carry out
investigations. Heron teachers collaborate on curriculum strategies and
events within our own schools and are active in state and national
teacher associations. We bring a lot of ideas, energy, and connections to
our network.

What glue holds the teachers together? Most of us are graduates of
the University of Wisconsin-Madison, where we learned a vision of progressive practice. Several strong friendships predate our network, and
at least half of us have been student teachers or mentors for other Heron
teachers. A third of the Heron teachers teach at one school that serves
a low-income, minority community. Perhaps most important, though, is
our need for each other. Our network supports each of us in teaching
to our heart's content.

By ourselves, we lack the resources to teach as we intend. Together,
we write grants, develop projects, share curriculum ideas uncommon in
our buildings, cultivate community partnerships, produce conferences
and publications, and create a context where authentic inquiry, community, and communication flourish. We learn from and support each
other. We have become a virtual school.

There are no lesson plans for teaching inquiry or for creating supportive teacher networks. Project-based learning requires imagination,
flexibility, boldness, extensive resources, partnerships, and hard work.
Even though our local school districts are exemplary in both allowing
and providing some resources for our network, they are incapable of
organizing our most creative classroom practices. Progressive teacher
networks function in a minimal space, with one foot in school as it or-
dinarily happens, and the other foot in school as we want it to be.

Helpful Tips

- Look for teachers, in and out of your own school, you enjoy working with and whose vision you share.

- Develop projects that can be done more easily by multiple classrooms.

- Discover ways for students from your different classrooms to present their work to each other—for example, e-mail, exhibits, videos, miniconferences, and journals.

- Write a grant that supports a project of your budding network.

- Find ways to schedule/fund some of your collaborative curriculum planning: release days, extended employment, action research, staff development grants.

- Whenever you do not get the funds you request, find a way to reshape your project so that you can do it anyway.

- Look for community partners who are looking for teachers like you—colleges, agencies, businesses that share your focus.

- Keep in regular touch via e-mail.

- Send copies of student assignments you use to other teachers in your network.

- Write about your classroom practices and share your writing within your network.

- Persist.

▨ Semester-Long Themes

David V. Buus
Moorcroft, Wyoming

Over the years, I have taught by the motto "Don't teach harder, teach smarter." This has prevented me from burnout, frustration, and stress. One practice is to center my room around two themes a year.

This way, I am not always spending the last weekend of each month at school putting up bulletin boards and classroom decorations.

My themes revolve around the latest "in" thing with young children. My classroom has been converted to an underground sewer for the Mutant Ninja Turtles habitat and to a swamp where dinosaurs roam. One of my favorite theme subjects is "The Magic School Bus," which allows a whole gambit of science ventures. I have converted my room to an underwater experience and have had life-size stuffed cutouts of each child suspended from the ceiling, representing astronauts free-falling in space. Other themes I have used are "101 Dalmations" (mathematical computation); the Cathedral of Notre Dame (self-esteem unit); a forest in which Pocahontas lived (Native American theme); the Lion King pride rock (circle of life); and the Mario Brothers (maze of activities).

The children anticipate the beginning of the year with a new theme. Previous students visit the classroom to check out the new theme. I must keep the curtains pulled and the door closed so that the children are surprised with the school environment for the new year. Only the students for the new school year receive a clue with the mailing of a letter I send to them prior to the beginning of school.

My themes are usually planned a semester in advance so that I have the summer to collect and construct "props." Local businesses, theaters, and friends contribute to the collection. Don't be surprised when you are shopping in a local department store and see my name written on the backs of disposable display cases!

When Students Evaluate Teachers

Maggie Lee Costa
Modesto, California

For me, a beneficial practice is to have my students evaluate me at the end of the school year. I tell them that anyone can prepare for and pull off a very impressive lesson for a visiting administrator but that the real critics of my teaching style are sitting right in front of me. I let them know that, from doing this process in the past, I became aware that some of my teaching practices really needed changing, and so I truly do invite honesty in their responses.

I also include a self-evaluation piece in this activity, which seems to give them a sense of permission to evaluate me as well. I usually write these phrases on an overhead and the students copy them. There seems to be more ownership if they write it than if they were simply filling in blanks. It goes something like this, and students may choose to remain anonymous:

EVALUATION

I have done well in _____ this year. I really feel good about my progress because _____ .

One area I would like to work harder in is _____ because
_____ .

A great and wonderful day from this past year I'll never forget had to be
_____
_____ because
_____ .

One thing I really appreciate about Mrs. Costa is _____
_____ because
_____
_____ .

If I could change one thing about Mrs. Costa and her teaching style, it would be _____
_____ because
_____
_____ .

My future goals include:

1. _____
2. _____

I believe that I will attain them because _____
_____ .

The feedback I receive from this is valuable. For example, I learned early on that many students thought I had teacher's pets. Others thought I had embarrassed them intentionally. I did not have either of these behaviors as goals. But when I read the words, I knew that I needed to work on these areas. Of course, the evaluations told me what I was doing right, too, and what remained significant so that those "great and wonderful" days could return the following years.

Succeeding With Language Arts and Mathematics Instruction

Arlene Arp
Avondale Estates, Georgia

One way I teach language arts and mathematics is to have an academic center time that I call "ABC/123." For 30 minutes each day, I ask the children to choose a work that involves language arts or mathematics skills. The centers are presented in an attractive manner that resemble play, but each center produces increased comprehension or provides a challenging skill practice session.

Many choices are self-correcting manipulatives. Each activity is presented to the whole class, and then I work with the children on an individual level until they are able to do the work on their own.

The work cycle includes choosing a work, doing the work for as long as the child chooses, and putting the work away. When the child feels finished with the work, she or he asks me to check the work, and at that time we go over any needed corrections.

On successful completion of the work, I praise the child and encourage her or him to attempt the next level of difficulty, if appropriate. If this work is not obvious, I will point it out. In this way, the child works at her or his own pace and level without the stress of comparison with another child.

The work choices range in difficulty from pre-K to second grade, and the child chooses the work most suited to her or his interest and individual need. If a child requires more guidance, I help that child make a choice that best suits her or his current educational need and maturity level.

An example of a "123" work is playing a xylophone on which the notes of a song correlate to numbers. An example of an "ABC" work is working with a "sound box" in which the children match actual objects to the beginning letter of that object. I put five different letters in each sound box, and the children get practice with matching the beginning sound with the correct letter, as well as with increasing their vocabulary.

One of the most important impacts of this academic center time is that it produces a classroom full of happy, well-behaved kindergartners who are interested in the work they have chosen and capable of learning independently.

Helpful Tips

Start slowly with this activity. You must either wait until your children know what letters and numbers are or label the work to indicate which work is appropriate to select.

We Don't Play School Politics

Frances Goldenberg
Chicago, Illinois

I have been in the same school since 1964, and it has been wonderful. I went there as a child of 21, and I am teaching children of the children I taught. Hyde Park is the University of Chicago community, and the parents are very dedicated to the school. I have worked under several principals, and the school has been a great place to spend my career. The teachers are really very supportive; we don't really play politics. At our school, there are no plum jobs because we don't have any Title I money; we have nothing to fight over.

I do have some advice for the new teacher. When somebody asks you how things are going, smile and say fine. Everybody knows it can't be so. I have never worked in any other profession, but I bet it's true in business. I bet it's true all over. You have to appear as if you are doing great, as if everything is fine. Then, after a while, you get to know someone. You know who you can go to for answers to your questions.

If you have a friend outside the school, you can ask that person. Within the school, you will probably find somebody soon who can give you some tips. But truly, some things you have to go through yourself.

A teacher stays up all night making lesson plans for wonderful lessons and then goes in front of a class. What happens? The children talk.

The teacher is lucky if that's all the children do. You come into a class-room well prepared, and the class couldn't care less. How do you deal with that? You just have to go through it. Maybe you're lucky if you had three little brothers you bossed around. Maybe that prepared you a little.

Conclusion

This publication began with the expectation of approximately 125 pages of submissions and tips from a handful of award-winning educators. Because of the teachers' overwhelming desire to share, however, this book blossomed way past that.

The sole purpose of this book was to connect: teachers with each other, teachers to lessons, and lessons to students. I do hope this happened for you.

About the Contributors

Suzy Ables, Kindergarten Teacher
Huber Ridge Elementary School
5757 Buenos Aires Blvd.
Westerville, Ohio 43082
School Telephone: (614) 895-6070

Awards: Teacher Achievement Award, Ashland Inc., 1997

Lenora Deas Akhibi, Kindergarten Teacher
William K. Sullivan Elementary School
8255 S. Houston Ave.
Chicago, Illinois 60617
School Telephone: (773) 535-6585

Awards: South Chicago Chamber of Commerce Educator of
the Year, 1996
Kohl/McCormick Foundation Early Childhood
Teaching Award, 1996

Joan L. Anthony, Elementary Teacher
Hillrise Elementary School
400 Hopper St.
Elkhorn, Nebraska 68022
E-Mail: janthony@esu3.esu3.k12.ne.us

Awards: Presidential Award for Excellence in Mathematics and
Science Teaching, 1996
Cad L. White Educator of the Year, Elkhorn Public
Schools, 1996

Arlene Arp, Kindergarten Teacher
Avondale Elementary School
10 Lakeshore Dr.
Avondale Estates, Georgia 30002-1499
School Telephone: (404) 294-5324

Awards: National Board for Professional Teaching Standards
Certificate, 1996
Golden Apple Award, 1993

Carol B. Avila, First-Grade Teacher
Main Street School
679 Main St.
Warren, Rhode Island 02885
E-mail: ride0330@ride.ri.net

Awards: Rhode Island Foundation "Teachers and Technology"
Teacher Trainer, 1997
National Educator Award, Milken Family Foundation, 1996
Presidential Award for Excellence in Mathematics and
Science Teaching, 1995

Nancy E. Baker, First-Grade Teacher
Petersburg Elementary School
326 N. Arnold St.
P.O. Box 428
Pageland, South Carolina 29728
School Telephone: (843) 672-6241

Awards: South Carolina Teacher of the Year, 1998, 1999
Presidential Science Finalist, 1997
South Carolina Distinguished Reading Teacher,
International Reading Association, 1996

Carla Becker, Multiage Classroom Teacher, Grades 3-5
Norwalk Lab School
906 School Ave.
Norwalk, Iowa 50211
School Telephone: (515) 981-9370

Awards: Iowa Teacher of the Year Finalist, 1997

Patricia R. Bell, Fourth-Grade Teacher
Shepardson Elementary School
1501 Springwood Dr.
Fort Collins, Colorado 80525
E-mail: prbell@psd.k12.co.us

Awards: Mission Mathematics, National Council of Teachers
of Mathematics/NASA, 1997
Outstanding Elementary Mathematics Educator,
Colorado Council of Teachers of Mathematics, 1990
National Educator Award, Milken Family Foundation, 1989

Nancy Ann Belsky, Mathematics Teacher, Grades 5-8
Westmoreland School
40 Glege Rd.
Westmoreland, New Hampshire 03467
E-mail: nbelsky@westmoreland.kl2.nh.us (during school year only)

Awards: NCTM/NASA Mission Mathematics Writing Team, 1996-97
Presidential Award for Excellence in Mathematics
Teaching, 1991
State Farm Good Neighbor Award for Mathematics
Teaching, 1991

Mary Bernard, Third-Grade Teacher
Turtle Lake Elementary School
1141 W. City Road 1
Shoreview, Minnesota 55126
School Telephone: (612) 484-2150

Awards: Ashland Teacher Achievement Award, 1997

Nancy J. Berry, First-Grade Teacher/Principal/Science and
"Creative Writing Teacher" Grades K-5
Columbia Elementary School
20 E. Columbia St.
Logansport, Indiana 46947
E-mail: naberry@cqc.com or ces@cqc.com

Awards: Disney and McDonald's American Teacher Award, 1996
Cass County and State of Indiana's Conservation and
Environmental Teacher of the Year, 1985, 1987

Leslie Wooster Black, Kindergarten Teacher
Bay Point Elementary Magnet School
2051 62nd Ave. So.
St. Petersburg, Florida 33712
E-mail: leslie_black@placesmail.pinellas.k12.fl.us

Awards: National Teachers Hall of Fame Inductee, 1993
Alabama State Elementary Teacher of the Year,
Alabama State Department of Education, 1992
Presidential Award for Excellence in Mathematics
Teaching Nominee, 1992

Juliann Bliese, Kindergarten and First-Grade Teacher
O'Loughlin Elementary School
1401 Hall St.
Hays, Kansas 67601
E-mail: jbliese@hotmail.com

Awards: Christa McAuliffe Fellowship, 1998
Kansas Reading Teacher, 1998
Kansas State Finalist for Presidential Award in Science, 1996

Linda Boland, Gifted Education/Mathematics Specialist
Paradise Valley Unified School District
15002 N. 32nd St.
Phoenix, Arizona 85032
E-mail: lboland@pvusd.k12.az.us or lindaboland@aristotle.com

Awards: Presidential Award for Excellence in Elementary
Mathematics Teaching, 1996
U.S. West Arizona Outstanding Teacher Award, 1991

Lynn Bonsey, Sixth- and Seventh-Grade Teacher
Surry Elementary School
RR1, Box 5095B
Toddy Pond Rd.
Surry, Maine 04684
E-mail: lbonsey@surryes.u.92.k12.me.us

Awards: NAASP/John Herklotz Award for Outstanding
Contributions to Teaching Democracy, 1997
National Board for Professional Teaching Standards
Certificate, 1995

David V. Buus, Second-Grade Teacher
Moorcroft Elementary School
P.O. Box 40
101 S. BelleFourche
Moorcroft, Wyoming 82721
School Telephone: (307) 756-3373

Awards: National Educator Award, Milken Family Foundation

Janice S. Catledge, Teacher of Academically Gifted, Grades 3-4
Alice M. Harte Elementary School
5300 Berkley Dr.
New Orleans, Louisiana 70131
E-mail: ahe@iamerica.net

Awards: Presidential Award for Excellence in Mathematics and
                    Science Teaching, 1996
                    Delta Kappa Gamma Teacher of the Year, 1996
                    Louisiana Elementary Science Teacher of the Year, 1993

Maggie Lee Costa, Career Education Coordinator
Stanislaus County Office of Education
801 County Center Three Court
Modesto, California 95355
E-mail: magcosta@stan-co.k12.ca.us

Awards: Crystal Clear Award, 1995-96
                    Rotary Teacher of the Year Award, 1996

Doug Crosby, First-Grade Teacher
Cherry Valley School
Polson, Montana 59860
E-mail: kiwi@digisys.net

Awards: Polson Educator of the Year, 1995

Barry K. Elmore, Music Teacher
Edgar Allan Poe Classical Elementary School
10538 S. Langley Ave.
Chicago, Illinois 60628
E-mail: Belmoose@aol.com

Awards: Kohl International Teaching Award, 1993

Rachel Ely, Elementary Art Specialist
  McGavock Elementary School
  275 McGavock Pike
  Nashville, Tennessee 37214
  E-mail: racheleely@aol.com

  Awards: State Farm Good Neighbor Award, 1997
         Nashville Entertainment Association Award, 1995, 1997
         Nashville Education Foundation Grant, 1996-97

Katherine C. Falso
  (Home Address)   900 Melrose Ave.
  Melrose Park, Pennsylvania 19027
  E-mail: kfalso@mciunix.mciu.k12.pa.us

  Awards: National Board for Professional Teaching Standards
         Certificate, Middle Childhood Generalist, 1997

William Fitzhugh, Second-Grade Teacher
  Reisterstown Elementary School
  223 Walgrove Rd.
  Reisterstown, Maryland 21136
  E-mail: LFitzh3265@aol.com

  Awards: Outstanding Elementary Social Studies Teacher of the
         Year, National Council for the Social Studies, 1997
         Distinguished Teaching Award, National Council for
         Geographic Education, 1995

Susan Gabbard, Visual Art Teacher
  Nichols Hills Elementary School
  1301 W. Wilshire
  Oklahoma City, Oklahoma 73116
  School Telephone: (405) 841-3160

  Awards: Oklahoma Art Educator of the Year, Oklahoma Art
         Education Association, 1998
         Excellent Educator Nominee, Oklahoma City Public
         Schools Foundation, 1997
         Outstanding Visual Art Teacher, American Teacher
         Awards, Walt Disney Company and McDonald's
         Corporation, 1996

Addie Gaines, Kindergarten Teacher
Seneca Elementary School
P.O. Box 469
Seneca, Missouri 64865
E-mail: againes@netins.net

Awards: "Magnify Mathematics Through Music," 1997-98
"Celebrating Diversity Through Children's Literature,"
1996-97
"Loving Literature, Learning Literacy," 1992-93

Susan K. Giroux, First-Grade Teacher
Heritage Elementary School
2815 Highlands Ln.
Wilmington, Delaware 19808
E-mail: skgiroux@aol.com

Awards: National Board for Professional Teaching Standards
Certificate, 1997

Frances Goldenberg, Fourth-Grade Teacher
William H. Ray Elementary School
5631 S. Kimbark Ave.
Chicago, Illinois 60637
School Telephone: (773) 535-0970

Awards: Delores Kohl Teaching Award, 1987

M. Katheryn Grimes, Science Specialist
Frank Lamping Elementary School
2551 Summit Grove Dr.
Henderson, Nevada 89012
E-mail: katheryn.grimes@internetMci.net

Awards: National Educator Award, Milken Family Foundation,
1996
Presidential Award for Excellence in Elementary Science
Teaching, 1994
Christa McAuliffe Fellow, 1991, 1993

Catherine B. Harper, Second-Grade Teacher
Tangier Smith Elementary School
Blanco Dr.
Mastic Beach, New Jersey 11951
School Telephone: (516) 874-1342

Awards: Sam's Club Teacher of the Year Award, 1997
American Teacher Award, Walt Disney Company and
McDonald's Corporation, 1996
Hofstra/News 12 Long Island Educator of the Month,
1995

Robert Harper, General Elementary Music Teacher
William Floyd Elementary School
Lexington Rd.
Shirley, New York 11967
School Telephone: (516) 874-1257

Awards: Fulbright Memorial Fund, 1997
Adviser for the National Music Standards, 1993

Brenda Hartshorn, Multiage Primary Grade Teacher, Grades 1-3
Moretown Elementary School
Route 100B
Moretown, Vermont 05660
E-mail: brenda496@aol.com

Awards: Presidential Award in the Teaching of Mathematics, 1994
Outstanding Teacher of the Year, Vermont, 1992
Outstanding First-Year Teacher, Sallie Mae Award, 1986

Larry Hewett, Elementary Art Instructor
Chadbourn Elementary School
409 E. Third Ave.
Chadbourn, North Carolina 28431
E-mail: ce@intrstar.net (school), lhewett@weblnk.net (home)

Awards: National Educator Award, Milken Family Foundation,
1996
North Carolina Art Education Association's Elementary
Art Educator, 1992

Lynn R. Hobson, Resource Teacher
Maybeury Elementary School
901 Maybeury Dr.
Richmond, Virginia 23229
E-mail: lrhobson@aol.com

Awards: Presidential Award for Excellence in Mathematics and
            Science Teaching, 1996
            Gilman Award, 1994

Margaret Holtschlag, Fourth-Grade Teacher
Murphy Elementary School
1875 Lake Lansing Rd.
Haslett, Michigan 48840
E-mail: holt@voyager.net

Awards: First Runner-Up, Michigan Teacher of the Year, 1998
            Ameritech Teacher Excellence Award, 1994, 1996
            Great Lansing United Nations Association Teacher Award,
            1996

Loisann B. Huntley, Fifth-Grade Teacher/Assistant Principal
Uncas Elementary School
280 Elizabeth St. Ext.
Norwich, Connecticut 06360
E-mail: loisannh@aol.com or lhuntley@connix.com

Awards: *Technology and Learning* Magazine Technology Teacher
            of the Year for State of Connecticut, 1997

Rosemary Johnson, Fifth-Grade Teacher
Valley View Elementary School
2125 Twilight Dr.
Rapid City, South Dakota 57703
E-mail: rjohnson@rapidnet.com

Awards: Presidential Award for Excellence in Mathematics
            Teaching, 1996

Michael B. Kaiser, Fifth- and Sixth-Grade Teacher
Pine View Elementary School
2524 Corydon Pike
New Albany, Indiana 47150
E-mail: mkaiser@venus.net

Awards: Presidential Award for Excellence in Mathematics and
Science Teaching, 1996
National Science Foundation Award, 1996
National Teachers' Hall of Fame Inductee, 1995

Nancy Karpyk, Second-Grade Teacher
Broadview School
189 Circle Dr.
Weirton, West Virginia 26062
E-mail: nkarpyk@access.k12.wv.us

Awards: Ashland Teacher Achievement Award, 1997

Stacy Kasse, Fifth-Grade Teacher
Taunton Forge School
32 Evergreen Trail
Medford, New Jersey 08034
E-mail: skasse@aol.com

Awards: Humanitarian of the Year, 1988
Hands Across the Water Educator

Kenneth Klopack, Art Educator
Funston Elementary School
2010 N. Central Park Ave.
Chicago, Illinois 60647
E-mail: kklopack@mailgate.funston.cps.k12.il.us

Awards: Kohl/McCormick Foundation Early Childhood
Teaching Award, 1993

Fred Koch, Music Specialist, Grades K-3
Deer Path Elementary School
Cherokee School
475 E. Cherokee
Lake Forest, Illinois 60045
E-mail: fkoch@lfelem.lfc.edu

Awards: Friend of LDA Award, Learning Disabilities
                   Association, 1996
                   Kohl International Prize for Exemplary Teaching,
                   Delores Kohl Educational Foundation, 1988

Elvira Bitsoi Largie, Teacher/Administrative Intern
Newcomb Middle School
P.O. Box 7973
Newcomb, New Mexico 87455
E-mail: elargie@educator.mci.net

Awards: National Educator Award, Milken Family Foundation, 1996

Debbie Lerner, Multiage Classroom Teacher, Grades 1-3
Red Bridge Elementary School
10781 Oak
Kansas City, Missouri 64114
School Telephone: (816) 942-7821

Awards: Missouri Partnership for Outstanding Schools Award for
                   Project H.E.A.R.T., 1997
                   National Elementary Social Studies Teacher of the Year,
                   National Council for the Social Studies, 1995
                   Elementary Social Studies Teacher of the Year,
                   Missouri Council for the Social Studies, 1991, 1994

Tarry Lindquist, Fourth- and Fifth-Grade Teacher
Lakeridge Elementary School
Mercer Island Public Schools
8215 SE 78th
Mercer Island, Washington 98040
E-mail: Tarry_Lindquist@misd.wednet.edu

Awards: State Farm National Good Neighbor Award, 1994
                   Elementary Social Studies Teacher of the Year,
                   National Council for the Social Studies, 1990

Sharon C. Locey, Sixth-Grade Teacher
Riverside Elementary School
16303 SE River Rd.
Milwaukie, Oregon 97267
E-mail: clintsha@hevanet.com

Awards: General Elementary Teacher of the Year, Walt Disney
Company and McDonald's Corporation American
Teacher Awards, 1996-97
Oregon Teacher of the Year, TCI Cablevision, 1994-95
"Weekly Reader" Video Voyages national grand prize
winner, 1994-95

Kim Mason, Physical Education Instructor
Frank Tillery School
621 W. Elm
Rogers, Arkansas 72756
E-mail: kmason@rps.nwsc.kl2.ar.us

Awards: Arkansas Elementary Physical Education Teacher of the
Year, 1987, 1992, 1997
National Educator Award, Milken Family Foundation, 1996

Diane McCarty, Fourth-Grade Teacher
Price Laboratory School
University of Northern Iowa
Cedar Falls, Iowa 50613
E-mail: Diane.McCarty@uni.edu

Awards: Elementary Teacher of the Year, Iowa Council for the
Social Studies, 1994
Gold Star Award for Outstanding Teaching, McElroy
Trust, 1993

Barbara McLean, Library Media Specialist
Joshua Eaton Elementary School
365 Summer Ave.
Reading, Massachusetts 01867
School Telephone: (781) 942-9161

Awards: State Farm Good Neighbor Award, 1994
Distinguished Teaching Award, National Council for
Geographic Education, 1993

Sandra Miller, Fourth-Grade Teacher
North Star Elementary School
P.O. Box 8629
Nikiski, Alaska 99635
E-mail: smiller@KPBSD.K12.AK.US

Awards: Toyota Time Grants for Teachers, 1997
           Alaska Science and Technology Foundation Grant, 1997

Cindy Montonaro, Kindergarten Teacher
Huntington Elementary School
1931 Huntington Circle
Brunswick, Ohio 44212
School Telephone: (330) 273-0484

Awards: Who's Who Among America's Teachers, 1998
           Ashland Teacher Achievement Award, 1997

Richard Morgan, Music Teacher
Beethoven Elementary School
25 W. 47th St.
Chicago, Illinois 60609
School Telephone: (773) 535-1480

Awards: Kathy Osterman Award for Superior Public Service, 1995
           Kohl/McCormick Foundation Early Childhood Teaching
           Award, 1994

Cathleen Murayama, Kindergarten Teacher
Lihikai Elementary School
335 S. Papa Ave.
Kahului, Hawaii 96732
E-mail: cmurayam@makani.k12.hi.us

Awards: National Educator Award, Milken Family Foundation, 1994
           Primary Teacher of the Year, Hawaii Association for the
           Education of Young Children, 1990

Judith Olson, Instructional Services Consultant
  Lakeland Area Agency 3
  5253 Second St.
  Cylinder, Iowa 50528
  E-mail: jolson@aea3.k12.ia.us

  Awards: Iowa Teacher of the Year Alternate, 1997
           Iowa Exceptional Educator Award for Nutrition Education,
           1994

Kathi Orr, First- and Second-Grade Teacher
  Moretown Elementary School
  Route 100B
  Moretown, Vermont 05660
  School Telephone: (802) 496-3742

  Awards: Presidential Award for Excellence in Mathematics
           Teaching, 1996
           Outstanding Teacher of the Year in School District,
           1980, 1985

Sharon Papineau, Basic Skills Teacher/Title I Coordinator, Grades 1-6
  Washington Elementary School
  510–8th Ave. SW
  Valley City, North Dakota 58072
  E-mail: spapineau@fm-net.com

  Awards: IRA Award of Excellence, North Dakota Recipier , 1996
           Who's Who in Education, 1996
           National Educator Award, Milken Family Foundation, 1995

Tammy Payton, First-Grade Teacher, Web Editor
  Loogootee Elementary West
  Costello Dr.
  Loogootee, Indiana 47553
  E-mail: tpayton@dmrtc.net

  Awards: Internet Awards: Blue Web'n, Bonus.com,
           South Central Regional Technology in Education
           Consortium

Pam Peters, Kindergarten/First-Grade Teacher (looping practice)
Rossmoor Elementary School
3272 Shakespeare Rd.
Los Alamitos, California 90720
E-mail: Proftot@aol.com

Awards: CCAC Teacher of the Year (Credential Counselors and
Analysts of California), 1997

Sheri Radovich, Third-Grade Teacher
Holladay Elementary School
4580 S. 2300 East
Salt Lake City, Utah 84117
E-mail: slradovich@juno.com

Awards: Granite Education Association Excel Award Recommendee

Lesa H. Roberts, Fifth-Grade Teacher
Farley Elementary School
2900 Green Cove Rd.
Huntsville, Alabama 35803
E-mail: kenr@traveller.com

Awards: National Board for Professional Teaching Standards
Certificate, Middle Generalist, 1997
Huntsville City Schools Nominee for Jacksonville
State University's Teacher Hall of Fame, 1995

Lonna Sanderson, Fourth-Grade Teacher
Graham Elementary School
11211 Tom Adams Dr.
Austin, Texas 78753
E-mail: lonna@tenet.edu

Awards: Austin Independent School District Elementary Teacher
of the Year, 1997-98
Graham Elementary Teacher of the Year, 1997-98

Mark Wagler, Fourth- and Fifth-Grade Teacher
Randall Elementary School
1802 Regent St.

Madison, Wisconsin 53705
E-Mail: mwagler@facstaff.wisc.edu

Awards: Presidential Award for Excellence in Mathematics and
Science Teaching

Edna M. Waller, Fifth-Grade Teacher
Magnolia Park Elementary School
P.O. Box 7002
Ocean Springs, Mississippi 39566
E-mail: emwaller@datasync.com

Awards: Mississippi's District 5 Teacher of the Year, 1997-98
National Board Certification, Middle Childhood
Generalist, 1996
Presidential Award for Excellence in Mathematics and
Science Teaching, 1995

Linda Goodin Williams, Retired Science Resource Teacher
Centerfield Elementary School
4512 South Highway 393
Crestwood, Kentucky 40014
School Telephone: (502) 241-1772

Awards: State Farm Good Neighbor Award, 1993
Presidential Award for Excellence in Science
Teaching, 1991

Shirley J. Wright, Gifted/Talented Facilitator
Gate City Elementary School
2288 Hiskey
Pocatello, Idaho 83201
E-mail: wrightsh@d25.kl2.id.us

Awards: Earth Day Environmental Award for Environmental
Education, 1997
Idaho Project WILD Facilitator of the Year, 1991
Presidential Award for Excellence in Elementary
Science Teaching, 1990

CORWIN
PRESS

The Corwin Press logo—a raven striding across an open book—represents the happy union of courage and learning. We are a professional-level publisher of books and journals for K–12 educators, and we are committed to creating and providing resources that embody these qualities. Corwin's motto is "Success for All Learners."